GENERAL FREDERICK YOUNG

FIRST COMMANDANT OF SIRMUR BATTALION (SECOND GURKA RIFLES)

GENERAL FREDERICK YOUNG

FIRST COMMANDANT OF SIRMUR BATTALION (SECOND GURKA RIFLES)

THE LIFE-STORY OF ONE OF THE OLD BRIGADE IN INDIA : 1786-1874, INCLUDING REMINISCENCES OF IRELAND AND OF INDIA IN THE FIFTIES

L HADOW JENKINS

GYAN

Published by

Gyan Publishing House
5, Ansari Road
Daryaganj, New Delhi-110002
Phone: 011-47034999, 9811692060
E-mail: books@gyanbooks.com

Distribution Network
gyanbooks.com
India, USA, Canada, UK, Australia

ISBN: 978-93-6433-170-8 (PB)

First Published, 1923

2nd Impression 2024

Printed at: Gyan Press, Delhi.

GENERAL FREDERICK YOUNG-FIRST COMMANDANT OF SIRMUR BATTALION (SECOND GURKA RIFLES)

Author: L HADOW JENKINS

General Frederick Young

TO

MY GREAT-GRANDCHILDREN:

PATRICIA HARTWELL

DINAH HARTWELL

BETTY BARTHOLOMEW

GENERAL FREDERICK YOUNG.

From an oil-painting by J. REYNOLDS GWATKIN, 1839.

Front.

General Frederick Young

FIRST COMMANDANT OF SIRMUR BATTALION (SECOND GURKHA RIFLES)

THE LIFE-STORY OF ONE OF THE OLD BRIGADE IN INDIA: 1786-1874, *INCLUDING REMINISCENCES OF IRELAND AND OF INDIA IN THE 'FIFTIES*

BY HIS DAUGHTER

L. HADOW JENKINS

LONDON

GEORGE ROUTLEDGE & SONS, LTD.

NEW YORK: E. P. DUTTON & CO.

1923

PREFACE

It is quite necessary that anyone who wishes to understand these sketches should read preface and prologue.

The original idea in writing the sketches sprang from my wish to leave to my great-grandchildren a record of my Father's services to his country as well as a sketch of his personal charm and character ; and this idea has persisted throughout, and accounts for the varied audience I seem to address when I consider the children—as they are—and the mature readers—as they may be—in the future.

In the years that intervene through the story of my Father's active life I have included personal experiences which may be of interest as they give true pictures of some vanished scenes and of some memorable days in the early part of my own life.

The prologue is a portion of this preface for it tells how, in my old age, I try to pay a tribute to undying memories.

I must here acknowledge my great indebtedness to :—

> Thornton's *History of the British Empire in India*,
> Williams' *Memoirs of the Doon*,
> *The Life of Sir Stamford Raffles*,
> Sir Charles Gough's *Sikh Wars*,

and also to Mr. Louis Tucker's verses on Umbeylah, 1863. I can find no trace of legal representatives of *Indian Public Opinion*, the paper in which they first appeared, although I have made enquiries at Lahore; I therefore put in my extracts with full acknowledg- of the source whence they come. I should like to mention that the obsolete spellings of places, as Palimbang, Deyrah Dhoon, etc., have been retained when written contemporaneously.

L. H. J.

PROLOGUE

They tell us, by some perfect art
We cannot understand,
Our slightest deeds on mortal planes
Are pictured in unfading lines
In unknown wonderland.
It may be things we would forget
Or wish not to remember
Not those that come with old-time pleasure
When pacing Memory's Hall
In the sweet silence and the leisure
Of the lengthening twilights
In whisp'ring, sad September!
For there are moments lightly sketched
On that receptive wall
That rise up veiled in smiles or tears
Pale with the touch of passing ghosts
Or tinted by the various hosts
Of changing human moods,
All coming at our call,
And softened by the years.
A wand'rer on the downward slope
To that eternal river
That bears us to the further shore
Would fain erect a cenotaph
Before she crosses o'er,
Bearing to comrades passed away
Who rise to gild her evening grey
With phantoms of Youth's morning,
To each—a simple epitaph!
In cryptic letters it may be,
Like old runes few can understand
Save those who hold the magic key
Of universal sympathy
And care to wander through a past
Built up of love and memory.

CONTENTS

" Il y a dans les bibliothèques de Province, des livres surannés et charmants dont les couvertures bleu-tendre ou saumon se décorent d'arabesques dont l'or terni évoqua jadis je ne sais quelle turquerie fantaisiste : le dos est fatigué et disjoint et l'on retrouve entre les pages, des fleurs séchées, des silhouettes de papier noir, et des écheveaux de soie dévidée jadis à même le cocon par d'anciennes jeunes filles. Ce sont les livres de nos grand'mères.

" Lisez—à votre ennui—se mêleront des sourires. Puis un charme montera de ces pages oubliées et si vous y réfléchissez vous discernerez ce que leur ont emprunté des sensibilités dont la votre est sortie. Que ne devons nous pas aux rêveries de nos grand' mères ? "

GENERAL FREDERICK YOUNG

CHAPTER I

English Settlers on Northern Shores: 1660

I have often wondered why people write biographies! And here I am hovering round the idea of doing something like it myself. In this case I think I have found an answer to the question. It is that so often I have regretted the want of family records, more especially as regards my dear Father's eventful life. Though some of his deeds are undying there is nothing extant in the home-circle to place them where his descendants can be familiar with them. Vain is now the keen regret that while he was with us no one ever thought of putting down notes of all he could have told us—notes that we would now give much to possess. But those are, alas! among the many lost opportunities of a long life. I have therefore to draw on my memory to produce a clear picture of his personal share in the great deeds of the early part of the last century, deeds which heralded the wide boundaries of the British Empire in India.

There is no doubt a great deal in this history that strikes a note of sorrow and regret, but there is one thing we must bear in mind—and we must not lose sight of this truth in all history—that great things are built up on little things, and that hidden corner-stones have more to do with the finished structure than the ornaments on the façade. These reflections have led me to the thought that when my voice is silent (and few of my generation remain to keep me company) there will be no one left to speak of these things connected with our family-history which should be held in remembrance.

My great-grandchildren, who may live to see the dawn of a new century on this changing world, may care to know some things that link them with the old order: things that will fade away unless the story is recorded. It is therefore with an eye to the future, when Dinah and Pat and Betty and their possible successors may be feeling back into the past, that I am jotting down some sketches as my memory paints them.

No doubt there is a certain fascination in knowing that one had even a great-grandmother, but there is still more in the establishment of the fact of a great-great-grandfather and, even beyond that, of forebears that link one with a remote time famous in the world's history.

The great-great-grandfather of the children to whom these memoirs are dedicated was named Frederick Young. The first trace of the family that I can find says: "They came over to Ireland from Devonshire about 1660 under the auspices of the Donegal family, the Chichesters having in their gift the advowson of Culdaff and Cloncha parishes. The Rev. Robert Young in 1661 became Rector of Culdaff. His first wife was Ann Carey, and, in direct line, the Youngs of Culdaff, through the medium of elder sons, alternately named George and Robert, have continued to be Youngs of Culdaff to the present day."* It is, however, with the great-grandson of the first Robert

* Since writing the above the daily papers, with other sad and tragic records of the times, tell of the wanton destruction of the two old places I mention in my narrative, Shanes Castle and Culdaff House. 1922.

that we are immediately concerned. He was the Rev. Gardiner Young, who married Catherine Richardson and had a large family of sons and daughters, one of whom was Frederick. Born on 30th November, 1786, at Green Castle, Moville, in the North of Ireland, he was godfathered by one Frederick Harvey, Bishop of Derry, a cousin. This was the boy who was destined to become a pioneer in the building of the British Empire in India. Frederick was fortunate in obtaining a cadetship in the East India Company—a rare piece of good fortune in those days, for selections were made with much care. Latin, Greek, mathematics, and foreign languages did not count for much, but a straight shot and good manners went far! The candidates, so far as one could judge from family and surroundings, had to give promise of being men—and particularly gentlemen.

Great was the wisdom of the Old Company in this matter, for it established in the eastern mind the fact that the virtues of courage, truth, justice, and honesty were essential attributes of the real Englishman, the man who was coming into daily contact with the people indigenous to the soil whose ideals of life had not been so cleanly founded.

In looking back to the records of history we cannot but note with deep regret instances of greed and selfishness in high places, even premeditated indiscretions amongst our greatest men; nor is it possible to ignore a Providence that guided the star of our country's fate and weighed down the scale in favour of an open, honest path, when sometimes it trembled in the balance. Our enemies have claimed as akin to their own what they call the *British policy of Clive and Hastings—right or wrong my Country*. Let us take comfort and pride in the knowledge that the strong under-current in influence spread by millions placed less highly, who lived and taught by example, was "right is might and wrong is of the Devil."

So, under the ægis of the grand old East India Company, Frederick Young was launched into life at the early age of fifteen, and he served his King and Country for forty-four years without a break. His brothers and sisters, with the exception of the two youngest, remained at home and led peaceful, prosperous lives, eventually dying in their beds like ordinary mortals. The two younger boys joined Frederick later on, and life seemed to hold for them an equal promise, but William was killed by a fall from his horse before he had realized what life meant, and his brother Gardiner died of fever in the trying climate and passed out of the family-history in early youth. There are two old-fashioned water colours of these two boys, probably given to their brother before he left home for the far country. There is also a beautiful, delicate picture of their father, the Rev. Gardiner Young, and a silhouette of his wife, Catherine Richardson. Of my grandfather I never remember hearing anything; but of the grandmother I know that her fine, strong profile is quite compatible with the tradition of her great courage during the old rebellion of 1798 when in the distant rectory, after having buried arms and weapons in the garden in the absence of all the men, she held the rebels at bay and inspired her timid maids with some of her own bravery. And not only her timid maids: I am proud to put on record that the embryo-soldier, whose fine career still lay hidden in the future, on this occasion emerged into his first action. The soldier-spirit of the mother, a gift not acquired but inborn, had communicated itself to her young son. When the rebels appeared at the rectory (*after her preparations had been made*) and demanded entrance to search for arms, a dear old retainer of the family (his name was Nicholas Grady) barred the door with arms outstretched:

"Sure no man will come in here but through my body."

But his mistress and her young son came behind him.

"Let them come, Grady," she said, "and look for what they want."

And as she led them over the house the boy kept guard between the rebels and his mother, ready even at that age to face any danger that might threaten.

Of course before he left home on his momentous journey he had many farewell visits to pay to his relations. I am not learned in genealogies, but from 1660 to 1800 the family had increased and spread considerably, and there were many branches all over the North of Ireland. One of his visits, I remember, was to Shanes Castle, the old historical home of the O'Neill. It had its ghosts and traditions and still possesses, I believe, the mythical halo. This little story of his visit there is impressed in some corner of my memory. I know he had a warm welcome and that somehow there were cousins there! He was conducted to his sleeping-room with the old-fashioned, curtained, four-poster bed, large enough to hold a family! He felt very small and insignificant in its greatness, but, really tired and pleasantly sleepy, appreciated its soft comforts. Just as he was sinking into slumber the curtains were drawn aside and an old lady in a quaint cap looked in upon him with a smile. He felt it an effort to be polite, so he smiled back and murmured a sleepy "good-night." She seemed to understand and without any attempt at conversation nodded her head encouragingly and withdrew, closing the curtains behind her. Soon he was in a sound sleep. Next morning he remembered his visitor and thought it might have been some old nurse who remembered him as a baby. At breakfast, when all the greetings had been exchanged, he said:

"Who was the old lady who came and nodded at me last night when I was nearly asleep? I'm afraid she thought me rude. I was too sleepy to talk. I want to apologize."

At once there was a stir and great excitement and to his astonishment the girls gathered round him:

"Oh! do tell us, Cousin Frederick, all about it. Did she really, truly, come and smile at you? You *are* lucky! She does not come often, but when she does it means good luck in your life and a safe home-coming!"

And then by degrees he gathered that only once or twice in a generation came this genial visitor, whose smile presaged such good fortune.

I do not know what the official proceedings of those days were, but it is on record that Frederick Young was gazetted as a cadet in the 2nd N.I.*, in 1800, and that on passing his final board in London in the winter of 1801-2 some members of the board said:

"How old are you?"

The reply was: "Fifteen on 30th November last."

"Are you ready to die for your King and Country?"

"I am."

"That will do."

He had passed.

This is the last letter that Frederick Young wrote to his family before leaving English shores. It is addressed to his brother:

* This is on my brother's authority.

"To John Young, Esq., Trinity College, Dublin.

"*Portsmouth, February*, 25*th*, 1802.

"My Dear John,

"I am quite tired of staying here; the wind has been contrary for this week past—to-day it is pretty fair but blowing so hard that I don't think we can sail. We had very bad weather coming from the Downs. We were four days about what we might have done in four hours had the wind been fair and less of it. I have been but once on shore since my Father left me and I believe that is about a month or five weeks. It was to the Isle of Wight where I took a walk, dined, and returned to the ship. We have got ten ladies on board and they are all as ugly as the Devil except one and she is tolerable. We never see them only at dinner and perhaps of a fine day they may take a walk on deck. I sleep in a little place with five other fellows. You can't think how thick we lie. Our cots are hung so, and there is a little hole for a window without any glass. We are very comfortable always—except in bed. We get excellent dinners every day.

"The boat is just going off so good-bye, my dear John, and believe me.

"Your ever affectionate brother,

"F. Young.

"Give my love to all my Dublin friends and Mr. and Mrs. Stokes, and if charming Mary Miller is in town give my best and most sincere love to her. John, I think you are highly honoured by so long a letter!"

CHAPTER II

A Boy Officer in Lord Lake's Central Indian Campaign

Praise Him who isled us here and roughly set
His Britain in blown seas and storming showers.
We have a voice with which to pay the debt
Of boundless love, and reverence, and regret
To those great men who fought, and kept it ours.

After he arrived in Calcutta Ensign Young went, as customary, to the Old College of Barasel. Here he met Abraham (afterwards Sir Abraham) Roberts. The two young men later on served together in one regiment, one as adjutant, one as quartermaster. In the adventures of this most eventful period was cemented a friendship that only death terminated. It will be recalled with deep interest at a further date.

It is on record that Ensign Young joined a volunteer regiment and was present at Balasor, but in the absence of all records I have his own authority for stating that he attributed his love and admiration for Lord Lake to the fact of having served under him through the Central India Campaign.

As all the old home-letters (and doubtless they were many, for he was a good correspondent) have unfortunately been destroyed, I am guided in this story by the names on the colours of the 2nd N.I. (to which my brother says he was posted) as being the only safe way of following his career—sometimes as an individual and sometimes as one in a crowd—until I reach the points where our own memories fill in blanks and are supported by authentic history of the times.

In fact I cannot verify the real regiment, so this part of my narrative is really a sketch of that campaign in which I know my Father served in his early career.

Among the pictures that have been familiar to me all my life is one of Lord Lake, and round it clings my distinct memory that he was not only a great soldier but a personal and valued friend of my Father.

And near it hangs another portrait of a man with wonderful, speaking eyes, a life-long friend of whom I speak further on.

In 1802 the Marquis of Wellesley was governor-general of India and Colonel Lake was commander-in-chief of the army. French adventurers, whose wonderful stories are worth reading, had taken service with Scindia and were amassing considerable fortunes as well as gaining power and influence in this employ. They were fomenting trouble in the courts, not only of Scindia but among the lesser chiefs, all of whom were anxious to free themselves from British restraint.

The Marquis of Wellesley organized two main branches of the army for the purpose of establishing order and security for the British provinces and a reasonable peace in their dominions and in the neighbouring states.

Colonel Wellesley (who became the famous Duke of Wellington) was to command one division, directed to the affairs of the Deccan, and Colonel Lake was in command of the other division, operating in Hindustan. You must remember I am not writing history as such, but I am travelling through real scenes that have a fascination for all lovers of true stories—stories far more thrilling in their stern reality than any work of fiction. In doing so I am also tracing the footsteps in success and disaster of one so nearly-allied to us and our family. In order to do this I must pursue the general road, only now and then touching in personal contact the individual in whom we are mainly interested who was nevertheless a constant participator in all the wonderful scenes.*

On the very day of the conquest by Wellesley of Baroach on the western extremity of the Indian Peninsula—29th August, 1803—Lake struck the first important blow on the frontier of Oudh, defeating the principal French force in the employ of Scindia under an officer named Perron. Colonel Lake had started from Cawnpore on the 7th August. On the 13th he encamped at a place called Kanouge, and on the 28th, being joined by a detachment from Futtehpur, he entered the Mahratta territory. Perron's force was strongly posted near Aligarh and no time was lost by us in moving up to the attack. However, the enemy retreated so rapidly before our advance that it was impossible to effect an engagement. Colonel Lake therefore took possession of the town of Coel and made preparation for besieging the Fort of Aligarh, to which the enemy had retreated. The resistance offered was so feeble that in a few hours the Fort was in our hands. The fall of Aligarh was followed by the surrender of Perron and of an officer named Fleury who accompanied him to the British camp. There was, however, another Frenchman, Louis Bourquin, who was more of a soldier than those above-named. Taking under his command what was left of Perron's considerable force he resolved to make a stand against General Lake's main body.

These hostile armies met on the 11th September about six miles from the Imperial City of Delhi. After forced marches in trying weather the British

* In the absence of all written records, on my Father's own authority he served under Lord Lake through the Central India Campaign.

had just settled on their encamping-ground when the enemy suddenly appeared before them in great force which continued to increase in numbers. On reconnoitring General Lake found the enemy were in an admirable position guarded by swamps on either flank. Nevertheless, the British commander decided to give them battle at once, only pausing for a brief time until all the infantry and heavy artillery had come up from our rear. Our tired force was exposed to very heavy fire and General Lake's horse was shot under him. The position of the enemy was so strong that the great commander felt the difficulty of the task before him, but with that military genius, which is the power of taking wide situations in a comprehensive glance, General Lake, by a feint-movement of his cavalry, misled the enemy, who, thinking it was a retreat, advanced from their safe position, and soon found a steady line of British bayonets waiting to receive them! When I say British bayonets I mean also *British Indian bayonets*, whose steady advance brought the enemy to bay and sent them flying in all directions. Our victorious infantry then broke into columns of companies, making way for the cavalry to pass through in pursuit. These followed the enemy to the banks of the Jumna where thousands perished or were taken prisoners. All the artillery and stores fell into our hands. Three days after the battle Louis Bourquin and four other officers gave themselves up; the City of Delhi was evacuated by the forces of Scindia and the French mercenaries; and the British stood as conquerors in the Imperial City of the Great Moguls.

At this moment we look back to a scene of one hundred and eighteen years ago in which Frederick Young in his seventeenth year bore a part. And at this important juncture I would pause for a retrospective thought—for indeed we should never forget how, in the long interval between then and now, the very dust of Delhi has in part become holy ground by the scattered remains of the continuous successors to that "Old Brigade" whose gallant spirits still live in proud memories though their ashes lie far from their native land.

> "For it is on the bones of the English
> That the English flag is stayed."

Before we leave the precincts of this ancient city we must note what was found there. And surely this is the moment for every British heart to raise a hymn of "Te Deum Laudamus," remembering that it is no new or rare thing for our conquering armies to be greeted as "freeing the prisoners, and giving light to those who sit in darkness."

In this ancient stronghold of the Great Moguls was the last of them, now an old man, blind and miserable, fallen very low. Once upon a time as the gallant Shazada, or heir to the throne, he had fomented trouble in the land. But when Fate had gone against him and he was hardly-pressed he had been taken under British protection and generously treated. His restless ambition, however, prompted him to leave this haven, and he turned from his friends to their enemies. He joined the Mahrattas who undertook to lead him back to Delhi, but, as their guerdon, robbed him of all the substance he possessed, and, placing him on the throne of his ancestors as nominal ruler, usurped authority in his name, devastated his provinces, and left him only the semblance and shadow of kingship. In this helpless state he fell into the hands of a ruffian Rohilla chief, who, after subjecting him and his family to much barbarity and cruelty, which, as the historians say, "*surpassed everything known in history,*" with his own dagger put out his victim's eyes! Again the Mahrattas rescued him and inflicted full punishment on his oppressor. They again left him on his throne, but, usurping his power, ruled in his name, and, while professing to pay him homage as emperor in Delhi, kept him an abject prisoner with barely means to supply the necessities of life. It is not hard to imagine the joy with which he learnt that he was free and in the hands of his former friends. He demanded an audience, which was granted by General Lake on the 16th September, 1803. I quote from Thornton's History:

> "The heir of Timour, so long the victim of adverse fortune, seated in the capital of his ancestors, gave audience to the English General.
>
> "In that place his predecessors, clothed in the most gorgeous productions of the loom, had sat on thrones of gold, made radiant by a dazzling profusion of costly jewels. Around them had stood hundreds of obsequious retainers watching in mute attention for any expression of the sovereign's will; vassals from distant couutries tendered respectful homage and gifts worthy of his rank.
>
> "And now—how different was the scene! Beneath a small and ragged canopy, a mockery of regal state, sat one whose age exceeded that usually attained by man, but in whose appearance the lapse of time was less apparent than that of long and hopeless misery. While his name had been held in reverence throughout India his life had been passed amidst poverty, danger, and suffering."

Thornton then goes on to speak of his "ultimate misery, his blindness," but there I differ from the historian. He was spared the realization of the squalor around him, and perhaps in the clouded vision of his old age he still imagined that he bore the aspect of a prince-descendant of great princes. He could not see the pitiful aspect of his court, his half-clad, half-starved retainers. He heard the manly, frank voices of those who spoke to him with all the careful respect and ceremony to which he had so long been a stranger, and a compensation for his blindness was the merciful veil that hid the horrid present and enabled him to think of himself as once more a sovereign and dispenser of rewards. It would seem so, for in the plenitude of his relief he bestowed on General Lake a host of titles :—The Sword of State, The Hero of the land, The Lord of the Ages, The Victorious in War!

When our troops left Delhi Colonel Ochterlony was left there in a capacity similar to that of resident, and we may be assured that the last days of the old blind Emperor were passed in comfort, peace and security.

General Lake left Delhi to march towards Agra where he arrived on the 4th October. In the meanwhile the other divisions of the army under General Wellesley had won the great battle of Assaye and gradually the two armies were approaching each other. At Agra there were much parleying and sly, eastern devices to gain time (I do not think the word "conference" was coined then), while the English general quietly continued his preparations for doing effectively what he had come to do—take possession of the Fort and cut the claws of his wily adversary. On the 17th October, the battery being completed, the besiegers opened fire, with the result that in the evening the garrison capitul atedand marched out the following day. A portion of our force occupied the Fort.

About the same time General Wellesley's detachment had subjugated Juggernaut and Barabattu, thus procuring the submission of the whole province of Cuttack and opening the entrance to Berar. Our path, however, leads us to follow just General Lake.

On the 27th October he had marched from Agra in pursuit of a Mahratta force composed of some brigades sent from the Deccan in the beginning of the campaign and joined by the battalions who had escaped from Delhi. On the 31st October our forces were encamped very near the ground the enemy had just left. General Lake determined to push forward his cavalry. Starting at midnight after a march of 25 miles they came up with them soon after daybreak on the 1st November. This was the dawn of the world famous battle of Laswari. The details I will not dwell upon. The struggle was very great. General Lake's horse was shot under him. But the cavalry-bugles had sounded the charge, and, as the notes rang out in the short, silent intervals between the thunder of the guns from the enemy's lines, our men knew that those lines were to be won and those guns silenced and captured. All honour to the memory of the brave! They did it.

Those who understand these things will never trace the progress of this battle without a deep feeling of reverence for that indomitable courage and perseverance that led to success. "The dauntless heroism of those who fought and conquered at Laswari will aid to nerve the arms and brace the sinews of the soldier so long as these deeds are remembered."

Children and children's children, for whom this story is written, never forget that your great-great-grandfather fought there, for on its colours his regiment proudly bears the name *Laswari*.

After this great victory, the fame of which resounded through the country, the first prince to tender his allegiance to General Lake was the Rajah of

Bhurtpur, and he was followed by other minor chiefs who had ousted Perron at the court of Scindia. All the treaties with these chiefs were concluded by General Lake. Of course their history and details make good reading for the student, but it is sufficient here for us to recognize the fact that the Governor-General had now attained, through the skill of his commanders and the pluck and endurance through good and evil fortune of the armies they led, every object which he had started out to accomplish. But nevertheless the treaties with Scindia and Berar did not justify the Government in recalling its armies from the field. Holkar was now prowling about to create discord and give cunning assistance to those chiefs whose professions were loyal but not reliable. Negotiations were not satisfactory and orders were given to both divisions to resume hostilities against Holkar both in Hindustan and the Deccan. These orders are dated 16th April, 1804. And here I find myself somewhat embarrassed in writing my true story of the one subaltern in whom we are chiefly interested. From May to September, 1804, many detachments were sent out from the main body. Of those detachments the minor details are not given sufficiently to form any clue as to their constituents. I much regret the want of private letters and information. Some of the historical facts are very sad, and, in many instances, death, disaster, severe suffering and regrettable mistakes and failures followed them. These for a short time plucked a few leaves from British laurels, but never cast one stain upon the honour of those who loyally endured such adverse circumstances. However, they gave some confidence to a rejoicing enemy, and British ascendancy was for a time under a painful cloud; but behind that cloud its sun was still shining more brilliantly than ever.

But once more I feel quite safe in following General Lake when, in October, 1804, he marched with his main force after the illusive and continually flying Holkar. Holkar with his infantry and guns, moving with his usual celerity, had meanwhile approached Delhi. His army amounted to about 70,000 men, whereas the force left in Delhi to defend a city ten miles in circumference consisted of two battalions of native infantry and four companies of another battalion, the greater number of these being especially devoted to the protection of the palace and the poor old Emperor. In addition to the regular troops were a few irregulars, horse and foot. These at once deserted and joined the enemy!

And now again I run off the line to introduce you to a super-hero, a man who did not hesitate to take the initiative in disobeying orders, bearing the responsibility on his own shoulders when he realized the aspect of the whole question, and putting the honour of his flag before any thought of personal results. This great man was named Colonel Burn. He had been hurriedly called in from Saharanpur with the corps he commanded, to help in this great emergency. The orders given to him were: that the City of Delhi should be abandoned and the garrison devoted solely to the protection of the citadel and Emperor. The Resident went to him in person to emphasize these instructions, but Colonel Burn, seconded by his officers, was obdurate and determined *not to abandon* the city, and the unequal combat commenced. Holkar cannonaded without interruption day and night, and Colonel Burn, fearing that he might make a breach in the city wall, sallied out at midnight, and in a sortie with 300 men gained the enemy's battery, spiked their guns, and returned to his post with little loss. That was on the 10th October. On the 13th there were indications of preparation for a general assault. At daybreak on the 14th the Lahore Gate was attacked by a confident foe, but they were so bravely met that their efforts failed signally, and they retired, leaving behind them the ladders they had provided for their entry! That evening they made a show of assaulting the Kashmir Gate, but their reception was such that in the night the whole force departed, and all that was seen of them at daybreak on the 15th was their rear-guard at a considerable distance! This was indeed a notable contribution to British prestige.

Very generously and even enthusiastically did those whose orders *had been disobeyed* acknowledge the incomparable service rendered by this brave and distinguished soldier. It is quite certain that to abandon the City of Delhi, especially at that time when British prestige had fallen rather low, would in many ways have had so dire an effect that it is hard to say what might have happened or in what deadly peril it might have involved every British interest.

This is an interlude.

Having failed in his attempt on Delhi Holkar had invaded the Doab with threats to desolate the British territories.

General Lake arrived at Delhi on the 18th October. Transport-difficulties delayed him, but Holkar's threat in the Doab roused him to instant action. He at once detailed a force under General Fraser in pursuit and made his preparations to follow in person with his whole army.

He was first of all called upon to relieve the gallant defender of Delhi who had been attacked and surrounded by a party of Holkar's cavalry while returning with his corps to the cantonment at Saharanpur whence he had been summoned. With some skill he had taken possession of an old ruined Fort and was defending it against strong assailants. However the relief was easy, for Holkar's men no sooner saw the dust of the approaching English than they fled from the vicinity of the ruined Fort.

General Fraser with the advanced force on the 12th of November had fought a most successful battle in the plains round the great rocky Fortress of Dig, where the enemy, after severe loss, had again retreated, leaving in our hands 87 pieces of artillery. Our loss was severe and the gallant general was killed. Dig belonged to the Rajah of Bhurtpur, who, though professing friendship for the British and being bound by his treaties, showed the untrustworthy side of his character by firing from the Fortress on the troops of his allies. General Lake at once made his preparations for completing the glorious battle on the plain by laying siege to the great Fortress. This important undertaking was also successful. On Christmas Eve the British were in possession of this stronghold, and the year 1804 with all its varied fortunes and strenuous undertakings ended with a notable asset to British credit.

The year 1805, however, did not dawn with the assurance of peace and rest from arms that the weary forces would have welcomed. Holkar was incapacitated and fleeing in fear from the distant approach of the British. But the treacherous Rajah of Bhurtpur had to be dealt with.

On the 1st of January, 1805, the whole army, full of hope and confident of success, marched from Muttra and took up its various positions before the capital of the Rajah, and on the 3rd of that month preparations were made to commence the siege.

Of course it is not my object to enter into military

details; drawn away by its great interest I have perhaps already sinned in this respect. I need only say that all the circumstances connected with this strenuous operation add many illustrations of the unfailing courage, endurance, dash and indomitable pluck of the besiegers.

One little incident emerging from these reflections and holding its special link of interest is the recollection of an adventure which was personally related by Lt. Young in the declining days of his active life. It occurred during this siege of Bhurtpur. At a moment of desperate effort volunteers were called for on what was an almost hopeless "forlorn hope." But numbers came forward and struggled to the front. Among them was a boy officer in a native regiment. I can give neither date nor particulars, but anyone reading the history of the siege may note how frequently scaling ladders and temporary bridges across hazardous gaps were brought into play, resulting unfortunately in the loss of many precious lives among those so eager to attain the end they sought. This is the impression *that history gives*, but the story was told by my Father with a merry smile, with no hint of strenuous duty or act of daring, but as an amusing incident in his experience. On some ladder or bridge, no doubt struggling for precedence in the crowd, Frederick Young fell from a considerable height into the ditch below him. Here he was quickly covered up by all sorts of dreadful debris. It took him a considerable time to extricate himself and crawl out of his uncomfortable position. He had been given up as lost when he finally appeared among his comrades, a miserable object, covered with mud and blood, but quite uninjured!

That is the only pleasant thing I have to say about this siege. It continued actively and ceaselessly for nearly two months. In the end of February the batteries were played out and no longer usable; the troops were exhausted and short of provisions. The British force changed its encampment to another position about six miles away which covered the road leading to their depots, and there awaited events. After a long lapse of time the verdict of history is that the failure in this instance was undoubtedly attributable to want of strength. The courageous qualities of the besiegers and the confidence felt in them by their chief were in inverse proportion, both to their numbers and to the inferior nature of the artillery-machinery with which they were provided. For the moment active hostilities were in abeyance. Our army was weary of working without tools, while the Rajah recognized that Holkar had been incapacitated and could no longer bring him aid, and that without aid he could not hope to prevail.

On the 10th of March he made overtures for peace. After rather protracted negotiations the treaty was concluded by General Lake and his services were rewarded by a peerage.

Holkar, though routed on every occasion, still fled from capture, and was at large to carry on nefarious designs.

Just now there came a period of political *bouleversements* in the history of India.

As I am writing in 1921 I cannot refrain from making some remarks on the situation because anyone who has any knowledge of India must feel that an ignorant and false estimate of values is just now placing our Indian Empire in a perilous position. We shall recognize that this has happened before, but the merciful Providence which has always saved us in past times may do so again.

Sir John Malcolm has said in reference to the period

1805 of which I speak: "Though we must continue to govern as conquerors, it is our great duty to make our rule a benefit to mankind and to carry among those whom we have adopted the blessings of peace, knowledge, and improvement in all the arts of civilized life."

Pacific and economical measures were now to have ascendancy, and these were extended to the army of Lord Lake. "Scindia and Holkar were to fly without alarm!" This policy of allowing an open enemy to enjoy immunity from retribution *had not been the policy which had raised the British power to the lofty position which it had attained.* It was not the policy of the Marquis of Wellesley, but the blind and ignorant expression of the home-authorities. "The unusual talents of the Marquis of Wellesley were invariably directed to the noblest and highest ideals. He laid in India the foundation of peace, and increasing prosperity, and if the superstructures were not completed in accordance with the great design, the crime rests on other heads. The British government may pass away but whatever its fall or the length of its existence, the name and memory of the greatest statesman by whom it was ever administered are imperishable."

On the 26th July the great Governor had resigned, and as he signed his last letter to the directors of the East India Company a salute from the battery announced the arrival of his successor.

Lord Lake bravely combated the mistaken trend of the new *régime.* He went to the utmost limit in opposition, and a perusal of his letters and speeches shows not only his talents as a commander of men but also the clear and comprehensive views of a statesman who certainly knew, if anyone did, what he was talking about.

He retired in 1806 and when he died two years afterwards, whatever his opponents might have thought, the English nation marked its approval of all he had done for crown and country. Personally loved, and publicly honoured, he passes away from our ken.

CHAPTER III

In Java with Rollo Gillespie

What is the Flag of England?
Winds of the world declare!

The South Wind sighed
Never was isle so little, never was sea so long
But over the scud and the palm tree an English Flag was flown.
I have wrenched it free from the halliard to hang for a wisp on
the Horn,
I have chased it North to the Lizard, ribboned and rolled and torn,
I have spread its folds on the dying, adrift in a hopeless sea,
I have hurled it swift on the slaver and seen the slave set free.

During the few years following the stirring events I have recorded I lose sight for a time of the course of my Father's story. Whether he marched about with his regiment or was stationed at the depot; the details of Lord Lake's interest in and friendship for him; or the services on which he may have been employed: to all these I find no clues. One thing, however, enables me again to take up the thread of my narrative—that some time at this period he was appointed A.D.C. to Colonel Rollo Gillespie. And now on his own authority with the support of history I can follow him in the eventful course of his career.

And again I am going to touch on the history of our Indian Empire, because it is instructive as well as interesting to know why certain measures took a certain direction, while we realize the fact that those who in their separate individuality helped to carry out the great designs were the real muscles of that arm that kept Old England's Flag fluttering bravely in the breeze.

The disturbing and disquieting period after the Marquis of Wellesley retired from the administration of Indian affairs, and after Lord Lake, failing to impress the home-government by his remonstrances, had also resigned his post, was in some measure retrieved by the arrival of Lord Minto as governor-general. His personal influence in the episode we are about to record is very minutely given in the history of the time, and our interest quickens when he appoints Colonel Gillespie to the command of the expeditionary force in 1810 proceeding from India to Java. Colonel Gillespie was of course accompanied by his A.D.C., Captain Young. As an intelligent knowledge of the reason for this expedition seems desirable I will indicate it as briefly as I can:

In Europe the French, with whom we were at war, had annexed Holland and claimed the Dutch possessions in eastern seas. This endangered our commercial interests should we permit the claim. The French looked to Java as the starting-point of their eastern conquests. The home-authorities, as usual, recommended a timorous and short-sighted policy. They recommended the expulsion of the Dutch and the delivery of their arms and power into the hands of native chiefs, and the withdrawal of our troops!

Lord Minto foresaw—in his own words—*the calamitous and destructive consequences of such a plan to so ancient and populous an European Colony; the property and lives of whom would fall a sacrifice to the destructive sway of Malay Chiefs.*

With the initiative of a great statesman he decided on other measures, and without hesitation made preparations for them. Before doing this, however, he had carefully sought and obtained minute particulars and first-hand knowledge from a man who was well acquainted with all the circumstances, as well as with the history and geography of the locality.

Lord Minto's judgment, therefore, was founded on a careful base of knowledge. His informant was Mr. —afterwards Sir Stamford—Raffles, who eventually became governor of the island.

Although at the eleventh hour the Governor-General had received sanction from the home-government (the Company's directors not quite in accordance with them) Lord Minto felt himself in a great measure responsible. He realized that personal knowledge might somewhat modify his plans, and that there was great delay and difficulty in establishing communication between Calcutta and Java. He therefore resolved to accompany the Expeditionary Force in person. This gives us a little insight into the more intimate part of our own story, and suggests a clue to the "personal testimony" which is a great point in a further portion of our narrative.

The following quotation from a letter to Lord Minto from Mr. Raffles gives a necessary idea of the reason actuating this move; it was undertaken not so much in order to expel our enemies in our own interests as to release the native population from unrighteous oppressors.

> "The Dutch, solely attentive to their own commercial interests, have invariably adhered to a more cold-blooded, illiberal and ungenerous policy than has ever been exhibited towards any country.
>
> "In some cases the original inhabitants have been entirely extirpated. Wherever they displayed courage and magnanimity they have been hunted down with perseverance worthy of a better

cause. The Dutch claim to an established right in those eastern seas is very inferior to what has been generally supposed." And he goes on to mention "the prevalence of piracy and slavery."

The military measures having been decided on, the question of the route to follow arose. This area was very difficult for the sailing-vessels of that time, and cross-currents and adverse winds constantly prevailed. Mr. Raffles took the responsibility of contending that the longest way round was the shortest way to their objective: Lord Minto, anxious to avoid delay and having confidence in his adviser, decided to follow the route between the islands of Carimata and Borneo in spite of opposition from naval authorities. The whole fleet, consisting of upwards of 90 vessels, left Malacca on the 18th of July, Lord Minto leading the way in H.M.S. "Modeste." He arrived before Batavia on the 30th of July, and by the 4th August the whole fleet was safely anchored, no losses having been experienced *en route*.

The military governor was Sir Samuel Auchmuty. According to his despatches the horse-artillery and cavalry landed on the 5th and advanced towards Batavia. On the 7th the infantry followed them, and on the 8th the burghers of Batavia surrendered the city, the garrison having retreated to Weltevreden.

Though declining an engagement the enemy now made preparations for what the historian calls "passive resistance." A great destruction had been carried out on public and private property, but the small party of British troops that entered the city gave a timely check to these evils. Lord Minto's A.D.C. had been dispatched to General Janssens with a summons to surrender, but the answer was "he was a French general and would defend his charge to the last extremity."

Soon after the receipt of this message the enemy opened fire. Colonel Gillespie sallied out from a gate at the west side so as to cover the enemy's flank, and at once the firing ceased. Many lurid and nefarious designs were frustrated by Colonel Gillespie's judicious and decisive measures and our troops were thus protected from evil fate. On the morning of the 10th August a malay was discovered in the act of preparing to fire some powder magazines; he was taken and promptly hanged. The French proprietor of the place where Col. Gillespie was billeted essayed to show his patriotism by poisoning the coffee prepared for the Commander and his staff, but fortunately the design was discovered in time. The perpetrator in the confusion of the moment unfortunately escaped, and could not share with the malay that elevated position he had even more strictly earned!

That same day Colonel Gillespie advanced towards the cantonment of Weltevreden. He found the enemy had abandoned it but were encamped in strong force just beyond, defended by 3,000 of the best troops, four guns, and some horse-artillery. This force Colonel Gillespie at once attacked, and carried the position at the point of the bayonet, driving the enemy to retreat and capturing their guns.

They were overpowered, but not subdued.

They now entrenched themselves and their forces—greatly superior to ours—in a strong position. On one side a large river; on the other a deep canal; neither of them fordable. In the centre was the Fort Maastir Corselis, the whole being defended by numerous and well-organized artillery. These works had been prepared in case of emergency by Marshall Daendale, the French commander, some months previously. The season was very trying for our troops, and Colonel Gillespie on this account was unwilling to lengthen out the siege. He therefore made some preparation for carrying the works by assault. Some batteries were erected from which a heavy fire was kept up for two or three days with great effect. Though answered by the far more numerous artillery of the enemy we succeeded in silencing the nearer batteries and disturbing their whole position. At dawn on the 26th August the great assault was made; the struggle was prolonged and very strenuous, but eventually the Fort was taken. Just on the eve of capture a terrific explosion took place of the powder-magazines of one of the redoubts. Many men and officers, who were closely following up the enemy, were on the ramparts at the time, and there was a lamentable loss of brave and precious lives. My brother remembered that my Father told him: *I was blown up when in Java with Rollo Gillespie and given up for lost, but I came back all right.* For a long time I thought this might have been the occasion, but a careful perusal of the history fixes it at a later date—at which we shall presently arrive—leaving no room for doubt.

Our losses had been very severe; the actual combat had been so close that "almost every officer had been engaged hand to hand. Colonel Gillespie took in person two generals and a colonel and another colonel fell by his hand in self-defence."

The island was now really conquered so far as the colonists were concerned, but General Janssens still showed fight, and the Commander-in-Chief, Sir Samuel Auchmuty—with the aid of marines who gained several notable successes at different places—brought the gallant general to bay at Saltiago. Here, deserted by his native allies, nothing was left to him but submission. General Auchmuty's negotiations ended in the surrender of the island as well as of the French General, with all that remained of his army, as prisoners-of-war.

I must say I am sorry for him. He had done his uttermost; what man can do more? Looking round at the tragedies of life, and they are many, a fall like this comprises the most poignant tortures that a man of active energies, whose spirit still retains a throb of life, can possibly endure.

When all these treaties were signed, sealed, and delivered, Mr. Raffles became Sir Stamford Raffles, governor of Java.

But this campaign and its connection with Colonel Gillespie was not yet completed.

Of course this was called the expedition of Java, but it was in fact inclusive of all the Dutch possessions in that part of the eastern seas which had now lapsed to the French with whom we were still at war. To support our European politics it was necessary in this locality to uphold our own supremacy.

After the fall of Batavia there occurred a cruel and dastardly episode at Palembang in Sumatra. The Sultan at that place, alarmed at the reports of British successes against the Dutch, conceived and executed one of the most horrible massacres on record. Previous to these facts becoming known a mission had been sent to take possession of the Dutch factory at Palembang, securing the monopoly of trade in tin on the island of Banka on terms which were far more just and liberal and advantageous to the Sultan than those of the Dutch Government had been. This mission was received with contempt, and the English claims to succeed to the Dutch rights were utterly ignored. The mission therefore returned. It was followed by an embassy from the Sultan confirming the refusal. But before its arrival the truth had become known regarding his proceedings and vigorous measures were promptly decided on, not so much to assert our rights as to punish the faithless and cruel Sultan (whose plans were being carried out without compunction) and to rescue his unfortunate victims. On the 20th of March, 1812, a force under Colonel Gillespie sailed from Batavia. They were hindered by adverse winds and currents, reached Hawks Island on the 3rd April, and continued there a week at anchor. They were not idle during their enforced stay. Tents were pitched on land and numbers of men were employed in building boats for navigating the Palembang River and in preparing huts and other necessary things for protecting the troops during the heat of the day and from the deadly vapours of the night air. On the 10th April the fleet was able to proceed and on the 15th came to anchor opposite a channel of the Palembang River. On their arrival the Sultan attempted to negotiate through messengers with the Commander, but, his treacherous character being now declared, that officer refused to negotiate except in person at the palace of Palembang. Other attempts at cunning and plausible negotiation being frustrated the British commander was firm, energetic and prompt in his movements. Notwithstanding the excessive hardships that all under his command had to endure nothing abated their ardour in the performance of their merciful task. As they approached the strongly-fortified position on Borang at the mouth of the channel the terrified garrison ignored the orders of their Sultan to defend this passage and fled. We took possession at once and captured one hundred and ten guns which were found to be all ready, primed and charged! The troops were then re-embarked but fires appearing on all sides and rumours arriving of the carnage and destruction that was taking place in the town, Colonel Gillespie determined to push on with light boats, and try to stop the horrors that were being perpetrated. He led the way in a canoe with his personal staff and seven British grenadiers! The city stretched for seven miles along the river-bank, and presented an awful scene; an eyewitness says: "Romance never described anything more hideous, nor could the imagination create scenes more appalling." Amidst this reign of terror Colonel Gillespie boldly stepped on shore at eight o'clock at night with those who had accompanied him in the canoe. He marched with a firm step through crowds of arabs and treacherous malays, their poisoned weapons gleaming in the torch-light. He and his little band continued their defiant advance under "huge battlements with gateways leading from one area to another and presenting the frightful spectacle of human blood still reeking and flowing on the pavements. The massive gates closed behind them and their further way was like the entrance to a slaughter-house."

A malay pressed through the crowd. He walked closely by the Colonel's side, a large double-edged knife hidden in his sleeve. It was a dark and stormy night, but, in a sudden flash of lightning from the heavens, Colonel Gillespie caught the glitter of the steel, and turning round, regardless of the threatening crowd, ordered the seizure of the man.

The gallant soldiers had been followed by the men belonging to the gig and barge that had closed up behind his canoe at starting, so his party was slightly augmented. In all—seventeen British grenadiers, some naval and military officers, and a few seamen belonging to the boats. With this little force he reached the blood-stained palace-court. A panic had seized the Sultan and his excutioners—all had fled!

Having carefully examined the place, Colonel Gillespie ordered all entrances but one to be closed. There the guard of grenadiers was stationed. A strict watch was kept and in this dreadful place they awaited the return of daylight.

* * * * * *

The intrepid daring of a handful of brave men had awed the hundreds of cowardly murderers. The morning brought reinforcements who were unopposed and the town was relieved from further peril.

This daring enterprise gained us the possession of a very strong Fort and batteries without the loss of a single man.

The capture of Palembang by the ordinary methods of warfare would have cost thousands of lives.

The measures taken by the conqueror to restore confidence and order were so effective that all those who had fled the terror to the refuge of the surrounding woods returned to their homes, *or what was left of them!* There was universal content among all classes when they realized their liberation from the cruel tyranny that had oppressed them.

In a letter to Sir Stamford Raffles Colonel Gillespie gives a report of the transactions. It tells nothing of the brave daring that led to success, but details the causes which made the action imperative. In the eyes of posterity the conduct of this affair raises those who took part in it to the highest point, in admiration of that disregard of self which leads men through death and danger to noble duty *coute que coute.*

"To the HONBLE. T. S. RAFFLES,
"Lt.-Governor, etc.

"HONOURABLE SIR,

". . . You are not ignorant that Pangerang Ratov the eldest son of the late Sultan was one of the most abominable and unprincipled villains that ever disgraced humanity. It is to this iniquitous monster that the massacre of the Dutch may be attributed: it is to the indulgence of his vicious propensities that his father is now indebted for banishment and degradation. . . ."

The letter continues to give full details of the horrors we have recounted.

On the 20th May Colonel Gillespie made his final report of the "ulterior measures" he had adopted in placing:

"Ratov Ahmed Nujm-Ood-deen on the throne in place of his brother Mahomed Balruddin who has been deposed."

The report concludes with an account of the ceremonies observed in installing the new Sultan. They were conducted with every mark of respect and consideration amidst a crowd of deeply-affected and grateful people. The last paragraph assures the Lt.-Governor that the *cession of Banca and Biliter* is now complete and the treaties with the East India Company satisfactorily confirmed.*

There was no wireless or telephonic communication in those days—postal and transit arrangements were tedious and slow—but, given a man and a task to accomplish, and the thing was done! In a little

* Now known as Banka and Billiton.

more than a month, from the 15th of April to the 20th of May, Colonel Gillespie had quelled an insurrection of an appalling nature, deposed a king, and had a brilliant coronation of his successor. He asked no questions, he just did it!

And now we must return to Sir Stamford Raffles and explain a new situation.

The Dutch and French Colonists were subjugated, but content and at peace.

Java itself, however, remained rather unsettled. The most turbulent of the native princes was the Sultan of Jokjokarta. His reception of the British Governor at his court was most unpleasing. Nevertheless he concluded the treaties, acknowledging the supremacy of Britain and transferring to the Company all the usual privileges. This was before the expedition of Palembang. The departure of the troops on this occasion seemed to give an opportunity for the prosecution of certain designs. He had, in fact, been secretly working to establish a sort of Union, or General Confederation, of all the minor native powers to banish their formidable foe and circumvent the destruction of all foreigners, sweeping from the island of Java every vestige of European power. Sir Stamford Raffles, having had his suspicions aroused and confirmed, was in much perplexity as to immediate action.

At this supreme moment of danger and uncertainty Colonel Gillespie fortunately returned from Palembang.

He had embarked on a small schooner with his staff, had experienced a difficult passage—narrowly escaping shipwreck—and had arrived at Batavia on the 1st June, 1812. No whit discouraged or subdued by all his terrible experiences, his active zeal only required the stimulus of danger. The troops and large vessels that had accompanied him to Palembang were struggling against the difficulties that had delayed him, and could not be expected to arrive for some time. Sir Stamford had gone on to Samarang, and on the 6th June General Gillespie set out overland to join him, realizing from all he heard that delay was not only undesirable but absolutely dangerous.

With all the force they were able to collect the Lt.-Governor himself accompanied Colonel Gillespie to Jokjokarta where they arrived on the 19th June. The Sultan had sent out strong bodies of cavalry to intercept our communications in the rear, and to destroy bridges and lay waste the country. But the British commander before making any advance set out in person with a few dragoons to reconnoitre the position. He found himself faced by a strong body of horse, and, never neglecting an opportunity of gaining his ends by pacific means, he tried to persuade these warriors to return to the palace. He was seconded by Mr. Crawford, the political resident who acted as interpreter. But they met with a decided refusal. After more parleyings with the civil authorities, which only had the result of renewing the opportunities for impertinent refusal, Colonel Gillespie convinced Sir Stamford that the principle of lenity would only serve to lessen our prestige and injure the colony. Therefore on the 18th we commenced a cannonade from the Fort (which we occupied) on the *craton* or palace. During the 19th this cannonade was returned and no symptoms of concession appeared. Our force was exceedingly small, "not exceeding 600 firelocks and about double that number in dragoons, artillery and sepoys. Part of our ammunition had been cut off, and nothing remained but an assault."

This account is given in a private letter to Lord

Minto from Captain T. O. Travers, assistant secretary, Military Department in Java.

"In order to estimate the services performed by our small force, I should mention that the Craton is fortified: is three miles in circumference, surrounded by a wide ditch with a wall 45 feet high, and defended by bastions and ramparts all round.

"Other walls and drawbridges defended the approach. At the period of the assault it was calculated that there were not less than 11,000 armed men in the Craton, while large parties of three and four thousand blocked up many roads."

Captain Travers continues:

"*Gillespie was himself.* The assault was made by escalade: we took the ramparts and turned their own guns on the enemy. The hereditary prince took the first opportunity to throw himself on our protection: the Sultan was taken in his strongest hold."

This assault was carried out in three hours!

The letter continues:

"I regret to say that Gillespie himself was wounded in the left arm—very severely but not dangerously. Our loss on the whole has been considerable. *Captain Young and Lt. Hunter were blown up and much burnt but not dangerously.*"

This, then, is the incident alluded to by my Father and told me by my brother as a mere statement without particulars, which it gives me great satisfaction to verify in this place.

The subjugation of Jokjokarta concluded our

struggle for supremacy in these islands. The weak and helpless portion of a large community wanted strong, just and merciful protection. This desirable state of affairs soon followed under the shelter of the British Flag.

Unhappily at this point there arose rather acrimonious dissensions between the civil and military powers, and Colonel Gillespie applied for leave to resign his military command. The concluding remark in Captain Travers' letter to Lord Minto seems to point to what became "a bone of contention," so I record it, though it does not concern us; it accounts for Lord Minto's expression of his esteem for a gallant soldier in the last letter he wrote to Sir T. S. Raffles before leaving Calcutta for England.

Captain Travers says:

> "Craton having fallen by assault it was impossible to make arrangements for defraying expenses of undertaking, consequently the whole plunder became prize to the army. It could not be in better hands, they richly deserve all they get. I cannot speak too highly of the conduct of the army."

Lord Minto expresses his view as follows:

> "It is proposed to appoint General Nightingale to take command in Java, and place General Gillespie on the Staff in Bengal. . . . An honourable and advantageous station is prepared for Gillespie, whose military character and services I shall always admire and venerate, and I shall always rejoice in the opportunity of testifying these sentiments by contributing, as far as my power goes, to confer upon him those honours and advantages to which he is eminently entitled as a soldier."

General Sir Rollo Gillespie and his A.D.C. returned to India in the end of 1813.

When Lord Moira succeeded Lord Minto in the administration of affairs preparations were completed and another campaign had actually commenced. Here very shortly we shall once more meet Rollo Gillespie and his A.D.C., though no longer an A.D.C.

In parting from Lord Minto and Java I cannot refrain from suggesting a subject of thought to anyone who reads this story. While we pay our tribute of admiration to Lord Minto may we not ask this question in the light of all we have recorded? If he had *blindly feared responsibility*, and followed the instructions of the home government, what would the consequences have been?

Surely "There's a divinity that shapes our ends,
Rough-hew them how we will."

CHAPTER IV

BRAVE FOES BECOME HEROIC FRIENDS

"The path of duty was the way to glory:
He that walks it, only thirsting
For the right.
Shall find the toppling crags of Duty scaled
Are close upon the shining table-lands
To which our God Himself is moon and sun."

On arriving at this interesting and very essential part of my narrative I find great difficulty; the situation is complicated even for a practised historian, but for an amateur to lead the principal actors in the great deeds just recorded into their new positions and preserve her sequence of recital, entails a compression of events requiring some skill. In fact, figuratively speaking, it is a track with large and important obstacles which must nevertheless be vaulted.

When Lord Minto returned to India after the successful journey to Batavia he found a very difficult problem at Headquarters requiring careful and prompt attention. An old "rift in the lute," due in a great measure to that tame policy—*moderate* it was the fashion to call it—against which the Governor-General had found it difficult to follow his own sound reason, had widened and increased in danger.

The Gurkha tribe, the most active and intelligent of all the peoples who had opposed our intrusion into their country, had taken the advantage this policy had given, and, not being more saintly than eastern potentates in general, had been quietly growing large and powerful at the expense of their weaker neighbours. Their methods no doubt had been Jesuitical and corrupt. Their aggression at last broke the philosophical or, rather, apathetic indifference with which the Government had regarded their encroachments. Their open acts of defiance called loudly for strong measures.

Lord Minto protested against adhesion to the course of policy that had been pursued, as *very* inadequate under the circumstances. He, being a man of action rather than of words, rightly deemed that treaties and parleyings, promises and broken promises with no resultant benefit, had lasted quite long enough.

It was, then, during the last year of his tenure of office that the preliminary arrangements for a new campaign had been sketched out. And the campaign had actually commenced when he was succeeded by Lord Moira, who arrived in Calcutta on the 31st October, 1814.

It had been decided to invade Nepalese territory at four different points:

One force was to proceed directly against Katmandu, the capital of Nepal; the second to take possession of illegally-acquired possessions in Bootwal and Sheoraj; the third to penetrate the passes to the valley of the Dun; the fourth to act against the western army of the Gurkhas.

Our interest connects us with the third division. The command of this division was given to General Rollo Gillespie. Its strength was 10,500 men and 20 pieces of ordnance.

To be eventually attached to his division, between six and seven thousand irregulars were to be raised by Mr. William Fraser, first assistant to the resident at Delhi, and when organized "to be placed under the command of Lt. Frederick Young to whose peculiar fitness for the charge the Governor-General gave his personal testimony."

The force under the command of General Gillespie was assembled at Saharanpur by the middle of October and then marched towards the Dun. The advance commenced with the seizure of the Tinley Pass on the 20th October by Colonel Carpenter, who had been detached for that purpose, and with him was Lt. Young who had been appointed to the command of two companies of the 53rd Regiment as a temporary measure.

General Gillespie entered the Dun Valley by the Kerrie Pass, and immediately advanced on Kalunga. On the 29th preparations were made for an attack upon the Fort. At first it seemed as if no resistance were going to be made, and shortly before daylight the batteries opened on the Fort with ten pieces of ordnance. If the plan of attack had been carried out according to arrangements the course of events might have been different, but, alas! *somebody blundered*, and the forces had to retire after a frightful loss in officers and men.

There is no doubt that, in the beginning of this warfare, all concerned greatly underrated both the character and the military genius of the enemy. The bold initiative that had been so successful in other instances required a far greater strength in support than that with which we were now provided. On this occasion, when the position was realized, reinforcements were at once ordered from the camp, but by the time they had arrived on the table-land —and this country was not a level plain—our column had been forced to fall back with great loss, as I have said.

The effect of this repulse, added to the impulse of his personal daring, induced General Gillespie to lead an assault with his little band, assisted by two six-pounders.

With his old regiment, the Royal Irish Dragoons, and some of the 53rd Regiment, he made the assault.

It was a failure. A second attempt met with little better success, and a third, alas! was attended by the worst of misfortunes, for when the gallant soldier, whose exploits we have followed, was cheering on his men, within thirty yards of their objective, he was mortally wounded and died on the field. His A.D.C. Lt. O'Hara was killed at his side.

Lt. Young who had accompanied Col. Carpenter was at the front beside his old chief.

Sir Rollo died in his arms.

So England lost "an officer who had rendered great service *to his country; whose career had been marked by a courage that fully deserved to be called heroic. The memory of General Gillespie received from the public authorities the honour so well deserved.*" But he had gone from the place where his loss was not easy to replace; and we may give a thought to the sorrow that loss occasioned in all who had followed him in stirring times with love and confidence.

It seems a strange coincidence that on that very day* the government of the country changed into other hands. I am only telling you a true story, but, as I follow it, it seems to me as if the springs had gone wrong—the machinery groans and grinds and runs on different wheels.

But Kalunga was still to be the scene of fresh misfortunes and discomfiture. Repeated unsuccessful assaults and desperate defences had, however, their effect. The garrison had suffered much from British

* October 31st, 1814.

fire; they were in want of provisions and water and threatened by pestilence; and so in the end of November they *evacuated the place*. We entered the empty Fort and its appearance bore testimony to the desperate courage which had animated its brave defenders.

The Fort was destroyed.

I here quote some passages from *The Memoirs of the Doon** which are worth remembering.

"A curious episode illustrates the spirit in which the Ghoorkhas met the British in this memorable fight. One suddenly appeared advancing towards our lines, right under the fire of the batteries, waving his hand as he approached. The firing ceased, and he was welcomed into the camp. It then turned out that a shot had shattered his lower jaw, so he had come with the most perfect naïveté to put himself under the treatment of the English Surgeon! When discharged from hospital he ingenuously asked permission to rejoin and fight us again!"

"Two modest white obelisks side by side crown the left bank of the Raspunnah Ravine opposite Kalunga, one to the memory of Rollo Gillespie and those who perished with him, the other a tribute of respect to 'our gallant adversary' and his brave followers."

"We may credit the tradition which says that, on abandoning his stronghold Bulbudhur, the Ghoorkha Leonidas triumphantly exclaimed in a loud voice: 'To capture the Fort was a thing forbidden but now I leave of my own accord.'"

"Kalunga *was never captured*. It was entered when evacuated and then razed to the ground."

* Now known as Dehra Dun.

"Gillespie's tomb is in Meerut, where he was buried—a high pillar surmounting a pedestal on which is inserted a marble slab:

Vellore. Cornelles.* Palembang.
Sir R. R. Gillespie
Djocjocarta.
31st October, 1814.
Kalunga.

"It was repaired in 1862 by his old Corps, 8th K.R.I. Dragoons."

The force of irregulars, of which the Governor-General had especially recommended the commandant, had been raised by Mr. Fraser as political officer and now took its share in all the movements with great success. It was during one of these life and death struggles that the friendship of Lt. Young and Mr. Fraser, of whose picture I have spoken, originated. In the stress of some close combat Mr. Fraser had turned aside, or dissevered, the arm holding a blade about to cleave the head of the young commander, thus saving his life! Not half an hour later on the same field Lt. Young had the eminent pleasure of putting his sword through another foe, "*right up to the maker's name*," he used to say, to save the life of a friend. They gripped hands on the battlefield, and Lt. Young said: "*Now we are quits*." Such incidents (as is still the case) were unnoticed, but the facts live in memories and so this lifelong friendship was established.

After Kalunga General Martindell, who had been appointed to succeed General Gillespie, had left the conquered valley of the Dun in charge of a small force

* This should be Corselis.

and had marched his division to Nahun. The Fort fell into our hands without any resistance, the enemy on our approach having retired to strengthen the garrison of Jytuk. This Fort was erected on the summit of a mountain of great elevation bearing the same name. It was a formidable position and the operations for its reduction very difficult and protracted. And here we are conscious of the alteration of the guiding machinery in the background! Minto and Gillespie were no longer there! Throughout the remainder of this campaign there were perpetual discussions and dissensions and men were blamed for not doing greater deeds than should have been required of them. The directing brains at Headquarters in far away Calcutta did not grasp the difference between warfare in a very difficult country against a very brave and warlike race, and warfare against the softer elements of the southern peoples, in a far easier locality for military operations. An ordinary perusal of the history—without prejudice, as the lawyers say—suggests that, as in the case of Bhurtpur in 1804, stronger forces and material would have helped the men who had to organize these operations, and who had, moreover, to bear on their shoulders the responsibility of the cost *in precious lives* either in failure or success.

Anyhow the main force before Jytuk remained unsuccessful for a long time, making every exertion in their power, while civil and military debates went on. The first unsuccessful assault was on 27th December 1814, and May, 1815, found the division still there. General Martindell had resolved to wait for reinforcement before making further sacrifice of men and officers.

In the meantime General Ochterlony's force was more successful. In many quarters the irregular troops had been doing good service under their different commanders. Only in one instance was it recorded that they had failed. A force under Captain Hearsay in Kumaon had deserted and fled to their homes, leaving him to be taken prisoner.

It must have been early in the year that intelligence was received of a force of Gurkhas on its way to relieve the garrison at Jytuk. Lt. Young with a large body of his irregulars marched to intercept them. He was *unfortunately* joined by several hundreds more, so really doubling the number of that force with which he had been working and over which he had established perfect order and control. This addition introduced a new and unwelcome element. Suddenly, a party of these outsiders being attacked and put to fight, the dreadful panic spread ; the whole force gave way and were routed by an adversary far smaller in number than many they had faced before, not exceeding, in fact, five hundred fighting men. The historian says: " Such was the value of the irregular troops though commanded by an excellent officer whose exertions were strenuously but vainly exerted to induce them to keep their ground against an enemy greatly inferior in numbers." This was hardly a fair way of putting it, for the value of some of these men had been continuously proved by many tests, but who can stay a panic ? Suddenly it comes, disorganizing bodies of men who the moment before had been in full possession of self-control, calm and brave and ready to face any contingency. An exclamation, an accent of fear from one man among many, spreads like a malign disease through the whole body. They turn their backs on the foe—and flee like a drove of sheep !

So it was on this occasion. Lt. Young and a few of his officers found themselves deserted and alone among the enemy. With taunts and jeers the little hill-men surrounded them and pointed to the flying crowd: "What?" they said, "you here? All your soldiers are running away! Why not run after them?"

We may fancy the calm voice of the young British commander as he looked steadily at them with his fearless Irish eyes and said: "I did not come so far to run away. I came to stop." And he sat down on the rocky hillside.

This was the straight way to the hearts of these merry men of the Nepalese hills. Oh! how well, after years of experience, we know them now!

With cheers they came round him and his companions, who were now their prisoners.

"Ah, you are brave men," they said; "we could serve under men like you."

These were memorable words.

It was some time after this that Malown had fallen into the hands of General Ochterlony's army. Its garrison abandoned the outworks and came over to the British, leaving their General Ummer Singh shut up in the body of the Fort, with a garrison reduced to two hundred. His escape or receipt of succour were altogether impossible, so nothing remained but absolute surrender.

Ummer Singh, Runjoor Singh, and Bum Sah seem to have been the three principal chiefs under the Rajah at that time and with them negotiations were carried out.

Introducing a personal note into this grave history I have a hazy recollection of the shibboleth:

"*Bum Bum Bahadur*"

which remains in my mind much as "Bony" might have done in the English nursery-lore of small children at home! Probably this general was responsible for it. He seems to have taken a prominent place with the Governor-General in the negotiations that immediately followed.

How long exactly Frederick Young remained a prisoner, I have no means of stating accurately, but I know that he was treated with every mark of honour as a brave foe and that he usefully employed the time. He became intimately conversant with their language, he studied their religion, their prejudices, their manners and customs, and gained their steady admiration and even friendship as a man among men. Thirty-four years after this his memory had not quite passed away and he was able to render useful service to the British Government in India.

All this time Lord Moira was still giving civil instructions to military men and General Martindell's long-suffering force was sitting outside Jytuk! After General Ochterlony had settled all preliminaries to the treaties of peace, orders reached him to supplant General Martindell and take Jytuk.

But, as Jytuk and its prisoners with those of other strongholds had already been surrendered, the order was rather belated.

And so, as far as we are concerned, the curtain falls on the strenuous period of brave struggle and of duties carried out with patient courage and endurance in spite of all the trials our gallant men had been called upon to endure.

A letter to his sister Barbara at the close of the campaign will show how reticent Lt. Young was about himself and his share in all these events.

"My silence has merited your displeasure—but I have had more to do and done more business lately than ever I did before. To speak candidly I have a great dislike to writing during the campaign because to have given you a full account of the situation would have taken more time than I was master of and to have written you a *half* kind of letter would have been unsatisfactory and would only have increased your anxiety."

It must have been about this time that there occurred a romantic event which almost reads like fiction: I mention it because I think it adds chivalry and honour to the life I am trying to depict. In some circumstances of wild warfare a native chief and gentleman was killed, and all he possessed was at the mercy of the conquerors. He had, however, faithful and loyal servants. With difficulty they rescued the women and children of his establishment, among them his young daughter. For these they implored protection from the young British officer whose straight and generous character was probably well known. Names, dates, and places I do not know, but it is on record that, soon after the campaign, when the chief's daughter had died, her motherless little girl was sent home to Ireland with an English nurse, and her education and upbringing were entrusted to my Father's nearest relatives. So this responsibility incurred by accidental circumstances was nobly fulfilled and faithfully discharged.

Of the little girl herself I speak further on from my own experience.

CHAPTER V

A Memorable Episode in Empire History: 1815

A sweet little Eden on earth that I know
Mix't with myrtle and rose and vine

* * *

The snows of the glorious mountains flash
Above the valleys of palm and pine.—*Tennyson*

(Slightly altered, with apologies.)

At the end of this trying campaign, after nearly sixteen years of strenuous and unceasing service, Lt. Young had his reward; and it is pleasant to leave the fields of strife and sacrifice and try to draw a picture of what must have been as near an approach to an earthly Paradise as any oasis that can vary the changing scenes of a human life!

In 1815-16 Lt. Young began his long and memorable work in the Dehra Dun, a beautiful and fertile valley on the frontier of our newly annexed territory in Nepal. It was in this place and at this period that there occurred a remarkable episode in the life of Frederick Young and in the history of Northern India—an event from which his beloved name will never be dissociated so long as the troublous waves of time leave untouched our Indian army.

In view of his position on the frontier and the reputation he had so well earned, many prisoners-of-war were placed in his charge, and the Government asked his opinion as to their disposal. Some friend at Headquarters said to him: " You are in such favour just now, you might ask for anything you want."

Frederick Young did not lose the opportunity. Perhaps as he pondered his reply a memory came to him of a scene on a rugged hill-side, not very long before, when the hearty tribute of a victorious enemy had fallen pleasantly on his ear:

> "*We could serve under men like you.*"

He replied to the Government:

> "Give me authority first to release the prisoners and tell them they are free men, and then I will ask them to volunteer in the Company's service. If they do—and I feel sure that many will—I undertake to raise in a short time a body of soldiers that will not disgrace you, or the country, or myself."

They gave him the authority he asked for. He went to the prison camps at Saharanpur, told the men they were free, and asked them to volunteer.

His own proud words were: "*I went there one man and I came out* 3,000."

This was the nucleus of that branch of the Indian army. Three battalions were formed from these three thousand men, prisoners-of-war released and voluntary recruits—probably men from the larger force of irregulars that he had commanded. Since then battles upon battles have been fought and gained for the British Raj, and fortunes have varied and endurance has been tested to the very limit. Sometimes in unexpected panics a temporary defection has been shown by our own brave British boys, but *never, never* has a Gurkha been known to turn his face from even certain death to inglorious safety!

The senior regiment of the Gurkha Brigade still bears the name of the Sirmur Battalion; it is always stationed in the Dehra Dun. Frederick Young was its first commander. He was given the honorary title of Colonel locally and a free hand. He chose his own officers, and, in addition to his civil work he took upon himself the onerous duties of the ordinary colonel of the ordinary regiment. But the word "*ordinary*" applies neither to the men, nor to their commander, nor to the routine of their education! How he loved the memory of those glorious days when, sitting his charger on parade and watching military manœuvres, a runner would come alongside and whisper the magic words:

"Sahib, sheer ke kubbar hi, sheer ke kubbar hi." (Sahib, there's news of a tiger.) And the Colonel would dismiss the parade, and he and his merry men would go after the big game in the jungle! How proudly he would tell the story of his beater, who obeyed the word of command literally in the jaws of death. The Colonel was on his elephant, the men had followed on foot: one eager young sportsman had forged ahead. Suddenly my father saw him stop and point his weapon. Realizing the man's danger should he shoot and miss, his officer called out:

"*Recover Arms*" (an obsolete order now). The man obeyed as if on parade, and, pushing forward to see what it was, my Father beheld a big tiger couched for a spring within a few feet of him!

These traditions still linger. Every recruit who joins the Sirmur Battalion learns first of all the story of its original formation. This was proved to me during the preparations for King Edward VII's coronation. The incident, though chronologically out of place, confirms my story of the time.

Somewhere about the year 1881 General Sir Herbert Macpherson, who at an earlier point in his military career had been an officer of the 2nd Gurkhas, told me that in his time the traditions of Young Sahib were familiar topics among the men. He said it was not unusual for the elder men in receiving some new order to say with a respectful query in their voices: "Lekin Young Sahib ke hookum nahi ta" ("But that was not one of Young Sahib's orders") as if it were a kind of presumption to add to what was already complete! In 1902 I heard that some of the men were coming to England with the Indian contingent to join the coronation ceremonies. Thereupon I made some photographic copies of my Father in his political resident's uniform, and I wrote to Major Watson commanding the contingent—I had known his father very well—and asked if I might see the men. He very kindly asked me to tea at the camp in Hampton Court. My brother laughed at the idea.

"Nonsense," he said, "eighty-five years ago! They won't know what you are talking about."

"Then," I answered, "they should be told." I made my plans. No one went with me but my dear granddaughter, Mignonne Hartwell. I think everyone thought it ridiculous.

It was a confusing place that camp at Hampton Court! No one could direct us to Major Watson's tent. It was already the conventional tea-hour and we were in dispair. I saw a little man in native garb walking smartly on an upper road. I was fairly good on my feet despite my 68 years, and I soon overtook him. Instinct had led me right. He was a Gurkha!

"Oh! yes, he could show us the way to Major Watson Sahib's tent." So we three walked on together. I summoned courage to talk.

"Do you belong to the regiment?"

"Oh! yes, lady."

"Did you ever hear of Young Sahib?"

He stopped a second, and turning faced me with

astonishment. Then he said: "Jung Sahib hum logon ke Ma-Bap ta." ("Young Sahib was our Father and Mother"—an Indian idiom.)

Then I told him who I was, and that presently Major Watson was going to bring me to their lines.

He did so, and I can never forget the enthusiasm with which they surrounded me: all eager to show their medals and ribbons and decorations.

The little subahdar brought me the book written in two languages which is the primer of the Gurkha recruit and tells how, as free men, they enlisted under the Old Company's banner! In the excitement of it the vernacular came back to me, and I told them how in his old age my father loved to talk of them and the jungle-sport they had shared in that far-away valley he loved.

I am so glad we went and have the memory of that meeting.

When I woke up—as it were—and felt it was time to go away, a little crowd of wondering people had gathered round us. The next week an article appeared in the *Pall Mall Gazette* of July 9th, 1902. I do not know who sent it, perhaps some reporter in the crowd. It pleases me and tells me this was not a dream:

"An interesting though impromptu little ceremony took place in the camp of the Indian contingent at Hampton Court the other day when, by the kind permission of Major Watson, one of the daughters of the late General Frederick Young presented each of the 28 men of the Senior Battalion of the Goorkhas with a picture of her Father. . . . To this day the name of Young Sahib is handed down from father to son and the first lesson for each new recruit is the history of the Battalion.

'For was it not written both in English and the vernacular?' said the Sergeant who brought out the book of regimental regulations to prove his words."

This is a very long interlude but it fits in. I may probably indulge in many more! If there is a thing that interferes with one's comfort, it is a long footnote. I think the interlude is preferable. A footnote draws you from your page and you have to come back: the interlude is more like letting in light on the scene as it stands. This is my apology.

In this beautiful valley of the Dehra Dun the young officer built for himself a two-storied house. (See plate, p. 64.) Frederick Young was an Irishman; he built a two storied house and forgot the stairs until he had finished!

Of course the idea was new to the aborigines in that simple, primitive time, when the thatched bungalow was the regulation dwelling of British invaders in all parts of the Mofussil. But the neat way in which the stairs were added did not interfere with the roomy comfort of the house. Perhaps, included in the original plans, it might have lent grandeur to the entrance! It did not, however, matter much, for the hospitable doors were open wide, and the fame of its generous welcome was spread to the four quarters of John Company's dominions.

Here lived, giving and taking joy, the first pack of English hounds ever imported to India. Originally purchased by, and maintained for years at the sole expense of, the C.O. of the regiment, the sport was free to all. A picture of the hunt, the huntsmen, and some well-known followers, is now, as I write, in the possession of my sister, Mrs. Harry Sparks, but at her death it is destined, by her will, to adorn the walls of the regimental mess in the Dun. It is interesting to think that the shadows of these bygone men and animals, who lived and rejoiced and knew that life was very good, may again face the light of that unique valley where they once had Name and Being.

The outline of Frederick Young's public life at this period should include the wonderful development of the natural resources of that fruitful land where literally the desert blossomed as the rose. For many years the hot, destructive fires of warfare had swept it to and fro and laid it waste, sacrificing all its natural riches. In the reign of peace both the valley and the people of the valley knew what prosperity and progress meant.

The following extract from a home-letter dated Sept., 1815, will show how immediately his services were enlisted on this important line, and with what an active, joyous spirit the work demanded was carried out.

"Nahun, Sept., 1815.

"I leave this on the 2nd or 3rd of next month on a trip of observation from which I expect the greatest pleasure. I am to make a sweep of 31 marches through a country little known to Europeans and abounding in all kinds of natural curiosities. I have got private instructions to take my surveying materials for a map of the country. I intend in the first instance to move to the bank of the Sutlej where it issues from the snows, then turn to the right and move along the bottom of the snowy range of hills to the sources of the Jumna. Can you imagine anything more delightful than such a life? I am as strong as a lion and fully equal to the fatigue. Thank God I enjoy the best health and I know not an hour's pain or sickness."

As time went on his raw recruits became trained soldiers. They were not merely ornamental. There were little turbulent groups of men round about, struggling to upset the order and legislation of that new *régime* that was bringing comfort, plenty, and security to so many thousands. These people had to be subdued and kept in order. The Sirmur Battalion and its commander had more work than military parades, and more foes to conquer than the grand denizens of jungle-strongholds! The following correspondence is an illustration of this fact. Unfortunately it is the only one rescued by the family from oblivion. Doubtless there were many more.

"To Captain Young,

"From Major-General Reynell, C.B.

"Meerut, 7th October, 1824.

"*Private*.

"My Dear Sir,

"Your welcome despatch detailing the proceedings at Koonjah* so honourable to yourself and corps and all others concerned, reached me late last night and has employed me so much to-day that I really have only time left to explain in this private way how very much pleased I am with what has happened. I have forwarded the whole with previous letters from Mr. Grindell to show the state of the district to the Commander-in-Chief together with a copy of the Division order, which I issued this day and a copy of which I desired the Brigade Major to enclose to you with the official acknowledgment of your report.

"I trust that it will satisfy you of my full sense of the ability with which you have conducted this

* Now known as Kunjah.

service and of the gallant manner in which you have been supported by your little Goorkhas. I really have said nothing in that order that I did not feel to be justly due. I have desired you to send me the name of any individual who shone more conspicuous than others; this may be difficult when all behaved so well. Of Mr. Shore's conduct too much cannot be said. I trust however that the manner in which I have introduced his name in my letter and order, as well as what you state of his zeal and intrepidity in your report, may attract the notice of the Governor General in Council, and obtain for him some gratifying mark of approbation.

"Believe me in great haste,

"Most sincerely yours,

"THOMAS REYNELL."

And with this letter there is a copy of Divisional order by Major-General Reynell, C.B.

"Meerut, 7th October, 1824.

"Major-General Reynell performs a most gratifying duty in acquainting the Division that a very brilliant service was achieved on the 3rd inst. by a detachment of 350 men of the Sirmoor Battalion under the personal command of Captain Young, supported by a party of 30 Palin Horsemen under the direction of the Honble. Mr. Shore of the Civil Service. This affair took place at the Fort of Koonjah in the vicinity of Secunderpore, in the Saharumpore* district at which a very formidable number of dacoits (robbers) headed by two or three notorious outlaws had established themselves after having seized a quantity of Publick Treasure, killed

* Now known as Saharanpur.

and wounded several Palin servants that were escorting it to Saharumpore, and committed other overt acts of outrage in contempt and defiance of the laws and government. These insurgents were found by Captain Young—apparently 600 men with Matchlocks and other arms—drawn up in order of battle along the front of the village and Fort. They were instantly attacked and as instantly routed. Those who did not take refuge in the Fort fled through the village pursued and cut up by Mr. Shore's Sowars: the troops having no mode of escalade prepared, were detained before the walls until a tree was felled, and a battering-ram constructed under the direction of Lt. Debude* of Engineers who, with his Asst.-Surgeon Royle, had accompanied the portion of troops detached from Saharumpore. The Gate was then forced and the place entered and taken possession of—after a most determined resistance from its defenders—by the Sirmoor sepoys, sword in hand, headed by their gallant commander.† In a conflict of this nature it was but natural to suppose that considerable loss should be sustained on both sides but the Major General is most happy to find that the insurgents have suffered on a scale of six to one. . . . (A paragraph, in praise of Shore's conduct who fought nobly and received two wounds, to be conveyed to De Bude and Dr. Royle, and too long to insert. . . .) It is to be hoped that the salutary effects of the punishment thus promptly inflicted will not only put a stop to any further disturbance in the Saharumpore district, but will

* More correctly, De Bude.

† It is interesting to know that the guns here captured, and a simile of the improvised battering-ram—marked with a silver plate presented by the inhabitants of the Dun—now (1922) form a trophy at the Quarter Guard of the Regiment in the Dun.

have due influence over other parts of the country where a spirit of plunder and outrage has been manifested. The Major General requests that Capt. Young will accept his best acknowledgment for the able and decided manner in which he conducted the service, and that he will communicate to the officers and sepoys who acted under his orders, the admiration with which he views their steady and spirited behaviour in their first advance upon the insurgents in the subsequent successful assault of the Fort of Koonjah."

It is a matter of much regret that whoever copied this from the original left out the "*paragraph in praise of Shore*." One story of Mr. Shore my Father loved to tell with enthusiasm about this intimate friend to whom he was much attached, and this is the proper place for me to repeat it, but, in a letter written to me by an old friend of later days,* it is implied that with regard to small actions among those hills anecdotes of John Shore were frequent. On one occasion he speaks of a walled town with a gateway that was closed, but the " first man to push his way through the wicket in the gateway was Shore and he (your Father) followed next and they were at once on their knees and blazing away up the street."

And again : " It was in one of these actions that Shore got a shot in the neck with an arrow (this too your Father told me)," (*and we are all familiar with the brave story*), " which he couldn't get out. When the fight was over he went to one doctor and then to another to pull it out. Each of them put him off with some excuse that he would see him later when he had more leisure, etc., and at last Shore realised that the wound was considered fatal—that

* The late George Mordaunt Ricketts, C.B., I.C.S.

if the arrow was withdrawn he must bleed to death! So he then and there sat down and wrote off his official dispatch to Government and when all he had to do was done, he faced his fate and told them to 'draw the arrow out!' To do this it was necessary to turn the arrow in the wound—it being almost in touch with the jugular vein was what the doctors had dreaded—but *it turned easily!* It so happened that it was not a fighting arrow."

This is George Rickett's account of the incident, but I remember a few further particulars. It seemed that this arrow-shooting tribe always carried a sharp, smooth, plain arrow in every quiver for practising at targets, and luckily for John Shore and his friends his assailant must have drawn upon him the reserve arrow, the last in his quiver! The fighting-arrows were all deeply-barbed and could not have been turned without inflicting fatal injury in this position, so by less than half an inch the gallant John Shore's life was saved! I think it must have been this incident to which Major General Reynell's dispatch referred—but I do not know.

And now, before I continue to say more of my Father's military occupations, I want to tell fully how important a place he was taking in all civil details during the next seven years. Not perfunctorily, but with all his heart and energy, he devoted himself to the place and the people among whom a kindly destiny had landed him. There are very few official records or long-winded statements. He just took the work in hand and *did it*—and never talked about it.

But I want it to be recorded fully here, although never in my memory did the subject form any portion of his talks of old times.

I have very carefully gone over *Mr. F. Williams' Memoirs of Dehra Doon** and I come to the conclusion that as regards the earlier history he is not very informative. All his data are from 1822 onward, just the time when what one chronicler truly calls "The halcyon period" of Dun history was merging into civil records, fiscal interests, and blue-book statistics. For instance, in § 361, there is actually a note of interrogation as to the origin of the Sirmur Battalion! Of this I have given the true story, on the authority of the chief actor, as related to his son, and to his sons-in-law, and well-known to all his contemporaries.

The "3,000" men of whom my Father spoke may not have all been prisoners-of-war—some may have been men who served in the Irregular Force he had commanded, or have come from other sources as voluntary recruits—but they undoubtedly formed the nucleus of those well-known battalions, the Sirmur, the Nurseera, and *I think* the Kumaon; and I have always understood the date to have been 1815.

And again, in §§ 496 and following, when government-officials talked from 1827 to 1844 about "*the advisability of cultivating tea*," they quite ignored the first little plantation that left otherwise its small record in the story of that time. It may have been that some early advocate of tea-cultivation drew the attention of the Government to the fact of a successful experiment on an unpretending scale in a private garden, and that this small affair called forth the dictum of the then-dawning (and I may say cloudy) Red Tape period of, not "Your money or your life"—in the frankness of the Highwayman—but "Your tea or your appointment." That is what actually happened: my Father gave up his tea-garden and the

* Now known as Dún.

Government took it over. There was no mention of compensation!

I never heard my Father talk of Tea—or of Potatoes—though he undeniably grew the *first potatoes in the Himalayas*, and *therefore* the first house which he built in Mussuri—and called "Mulliagoes"—was popularly known as "The Potato Garden." We shall hear later of the big men who stayed there with him.

The way in which his agricultural achievements were first revealed to me was somewhat amusing, and must form another interlude here.

When I was about 14 years of age I was taken somewhere in London to have my hair cut, but others of the party had precedence, and I was left to look at picture-books in a waiting room—like a doctor's room in the present day, only instead of illustrated papers (which were still unborn), there were old fashioned albums and "books of beauty." What engaged my attention was a book bound in maroon and gold-lettered, with beautiful full-page engravings. I was attracted by a picture of Mussuri in the Himalayas, and, turning with interest to the letter-press, read to my great delight of "Colonel Young's beautiful houses" and how "he had created a Paradise in a jungle-valley, and planted the *first Tea* and the *first Potato* ever grown in the Himalayas!"

At that time I had not long been away from my home, or my Mother's companionship, and I was under the fixed impression that my Father was really one of the most famous men in the world! So I took all the glory of it as a matter of course.

In that long interval of glorious "spacious days" the uncrowned King of Dun Valley lived a full life. Sport was of the best and unique in this way—the antagonist was not only "something to kill," it was a foeman worthy of the strife; it had to be con-

"THE POTATO GARDEN."

[face p. 64

quered and repressed to save weak and helpless human lives that needed protection, for the enemy abounded in numbers and strength.

Then there was his hospitality that shared all good things, and the benevolent thought and consideration for all members of the community, irrespective of class or colour. And also, in pre-eminent place, the service to his country conscientiously pursued from day to day, and his unsparing personal care for the officers and men of whom he was the beloved chief.

And there were other duties of a most serious nature of which none of us ever entertained an appreciative idea until, on reading to compile this memoir, I find the records of his wonderful past. It was a time of strain and responsibility that would have lined the brows of many men ; and I think how great must have been the inner strength that, through all the troubled waves of life, enabled him to be *what* he was in the simple, monotonous days of old age—ever the brightest and most cheery member of the family where, in the light that reveals the past, I recognize him to have been a *giant among pigmies*.

His work in the Dun dated from 1815.

This book, *Williams' Memoirs*, bears testimony to the fact that he combined the offices of civil judge, magistrate, and collector with that of commandant of the Sirmur Battalion ; and his own letter tells us that he was also a surveyor of the district on private orders ! His captain, Captain I. Fisher (his officers were selected by himself), was his joint-magistrate ; he had one lieutenant and a doctor, Lt. Kirke and Dr. Gray.

There are no existing official records that I have been able to unearth of the staging of this drama in the Dun Valley ; and the whole responsibility for the *mise en scène* seems to rest on the manager—Lt. F. Young, aged 28.

In later periods he is spoken of variously as "superintendent" and "political agent," but whatever title he held in those pre-record days, justice pure and simple bears testimony to his work.

> "Captain Young took charge of the Pergunah 1st April, 1819. The summary nature of his operations may be judged from the fact that they only occupied five or six days!" Well done Frederick Young! Let us look at the result:
>
> "In proof of the excellence of his arrangements the whole of the revenue for the last five years had been paid up: not even a *chaprassie* (peon) had been employed on Revenue duties nor had there been a single complaint.
>
> "Up to July, 1824, the system continued to work well: collections were all made without the employment of a single coercive process."

I claim this as a grand record.

When, after the retirement of John Shore, Major Young was appointed as his successor, it must have been rather a shock to some of the civil aspirants who were thus superseded by a soldier!

As this most interesting book (Williams' Memoirs) will be much read I feel compelled to draw attention to a minor point—but one of personal interest. Mr. Williams makes some cynical remarks about Major Young's letters "*being*"—as he says of one undated document—"*forgetful of date and sometimes grammar.*" Also: "*Major Young has rather a confused way of expressing himself.*" In this connection I ask the reader to remember that Mr. Williams speaks of a boy who at fifteen was living a man's life, in the far-off days when educational courses were rather slurred over, until *the man* underlying the boy came to the top and educated himself! Nevertheless I think all the letters quoted by Mr. Williams, and also those I give here, will bear comparison not only with letters of greater men, but men who also *did things*. Frederick Young wrote and spoke—*straight on*.

CHAPTER VI

Early Memories

Is it so small a thing
To have enjoyed the sun?
To have lived light in the Spring?
To have loved—to have thought—*to have done?*

In 1825, when my father was living in the Dun alone, a free man with no domestic ties, and discharging fully all the responsibilities he had undertaken, he made time to think also of himself! He then met the daughter of Colonel and Mrs. Bird and she became his wife.

As I have given a brief sketch of the ancestry of my famous Father, I will now try and trace the rather romantic story of my grandparents on the maternal side. Alas! the parchments that gave full historical facts are not in my possession as they ought to have been. They belonged to my uncle and godfather, my mother's only brother. These parchments and his gold watch and seals (which had belonged to his grandfather) passed out of the family because an old woman had no moral sense and was more greedy than grateful! They had formed one of the intense interests of my girlhood, and everyone knew of my uncle's intention that they should go to his godchild, his favourite sister's daughter. I can hear his voice now, and can see his old wife's acquiescing smile, as he said many times when I was fingering them on his writing table: "They will all be yours some day." But when his last hour came his wife was dead, and no member of his family was near him, only this old woman—a sister of his wife's, a widow without means whom he had generously supported for years. His ample pension as a general in the Old Company's service was of course only for his life time. He was not a rich man, but he left house and furniture and what means he had to this old person. I never saw his will, but it is quite possible that he never mentioned details and believed that his known wishes so often expressed would be respected, but all I could regain from her was my Mother's miniature and some family-pictures—my parchments and my seals and the old watch I never saw again!

I have always been ready for a fight when I realized, as in this case, the justice of my cause, but at that time everything conspired against me. At the moment I failed to realize all that this loss meant.

One of the great blessings that fill me with thankfulness is the memory that I am glad to possess, and so it happens that the outline of this little history of my maternal ancestry is gleaned from this treasure-house and is bare in detail because I record only the facts for which I can vouch.

After the French Revolution, among the thousands of refugees who, powerless to help their royal master and their country, fled from the murderous *régime* of Robespierre and his satellites, we may trace two separate families whose histories, beginning very far apart, finally merged into one and claim our personal interest.

The stolen parchments in which these separate and interesting lives were recorded thrilled me as a girl of sixteen, proud to feel that my forbears had had a part in great historical scenes of other times. Enough of these exciting records remains in my mind to make me feel what I have lost, but, as I wish to be quite accurate, I only quote the chief facts.

Attached to the French court for some successive generations, an Irishman named Bird held high office (the parchment gave dates and details). When the Revolution broke out his son was a young officer in those loyal Guards that suffered so nobly in their futile efforts to stem the storm. When all hope was over and they were helpless in the universal chaos, father and son, saving their lives with difficulty, ultimately joined the crowd of *émigrés* fleeing from the stricken land.

Under the name of Loiseau they found a refuge in the East Indies. Here after a time they made their home, and, with his brilliant record of service to the French court, Count Loiseau obtained a commission for his son in the Honble. East India Company. They quickly resumed their rightful name and nationality, and in due course the son became Colonel Bird, my grandfather. There is a portrait of him among the family-pictures. It has always been a favourite of mine. My admiration for him is not diminished by the record that he suffered from gout, used strong language, and had a fiery temper! I am sure he was a man.

Of the second family of *émigrés*, who sought refuge in India at the same time in the same circumstances, I know only the real name, and the one they assumed. So far as their remoter history was concerned, its record occupied a large space in these old papers and was deeply valued by my dear old uncle. They belonged to a branch of that large and widely-scattered family of de la Trémouille. Leaving their native land in search of safety they had assumed the poetic and symbolic name of Deshirondelles, or The Swallows! Of their story and adventures I can recall no consecutive record, but I remember that one thing the parchment traced which loomed large in my uncle's mind was some connection between his mother's family and that Charlotte de la Trémouille, Countess of Derby, who defended Lathom Houses (1644-5) in the absence of her husband during the Civil Wars. All that I can vouch for is that as time passed on the hand of destiny brought the two families together and my grandfather married Mdlle. Deshirondelles, giving rise to the feeble joke in the legend that in a time of banishment the Swallow married another Bird!

So Marie the Swallow became Mary Bird, my handsome grandmother. Whether they married in youth or old age, I know not—I think the latter. But the sketchy outline becomes interesting when we learn that in 1825:

> "Colonel Frederick Young, Colonel of the Sirmoor Battalion of Gurkha Rifles, married Jeanette, the daughter of Colonel and Mrs. Bird."

I do not even remember my grandfather's official position. I know he held some staff-appointments until his death.

No need to say anything of the personal charms of my father's bride; her miniature speaks for itself. (See plate, p. 160.) For beauty of voice and grace of movement I never met her equal.

For many succeeding years she was the worthy queen and co-ruler of the beautiful valley and its immediate neighbourhood. Widely known as a splendid horsewoman she shared her husband's love of animals. Her favourite chestnut arab is in the foreground of the picture of their home in the Dun. In every way co-operating with her generous husband in all his undertakings and duties and pleasures, she brought happiness and beauty and contentment into his home. Of those who knew them at that time the voices have long been silent, but their pleasant echoes still live in my memory.

Before I appeared on the scene in 1834 (December 25th, for I was a Xmas-present) four children had preceded me.

Catherine Mary, Eliza who died young, Susan Jeanette and Mary. The following letter dated October 30th speaks of the first event in the formation of this little family. My main reason for quoting it here is the further allusion to my Father's work in this district where he was promoting the "renaissance" in every direction.

"To Mrs. Richardson,

"Kalsee,* Oct. 30th, 1827.

"My Beloved Sister Hatton,

"I have taken up a small piece of paper only that I may not be induced to go on writing a long letter which, having once commenced, would probably be the case, did I not confine myself within certain limits. My reason is simply this. I have a good deal of business to get through ere I leave this place, and I am working at all hours to get rid of it, that I may return to my wife and child, whom I left last month at Saharumpore with her parents while I proceeded on a tour through the hill districts under my charge; of which I have been ordered to make a full and ample report in every particular. Nearly the whole month has been consumed in my tour with only one day's halt. I have hitherto only collected my materials and verified the information I had previously received,

* Now known as Kalsi.

and having arrived at the principal town on the confines of Jannsor, I must sit down regularly for four or five days at least to compile my report and complete my task. These circumstances must account for my letter being short. We have one lovely child, nine months old. God bless you and Tom and your dear children.

"I remain your sincere, affectionate and attached Brother.

"F. Young."

Then come other letters which I here quote in full as they give the best possible idea of the time between 1827 and 1835 and of the importance of the post my Father occupied. Of some persons whose names are mentioned I must add a few particulars which cannot fail to interest those who like to follow my story.

"Deyrah, 29th Dec., 1827.

"My dearest Hatton,

"I have too long delayed my promised reply to your kind and affectionate letter of the 11th May last, for in my short note from Kalsee I mentioned that you were not to consider it as anything more than an acknowledgment, and that the answer would follow when I had more time. I shall now commence by telling you that Jeanette, Kate and myself enjoy the finest health and all the blessings attendant on it. We ought to be, and I hope we are, suitably grateful to the Goodness of Divine Providence. The failures which have taken place in India and have caused so many individuals to suffer have not affected us. We are blessed with a sweet babe with whom no fault can be found in point of temper, health and appearance. We have the prettiest situation in India and every likelihood of my holding it till I am promoted to Lt.-Colonel! and then my views will naturally turn towards home—towards dear Somerset*, Colcraine, Magcosquin, Enniskillen, &c., and I may remain at home if I find I have money enough to do so—or, leaving wife and children, may return again to India, to reap honour and glory should anything be going on, or to get the command of a regiment. This, my beloved sister, is the bright side of the picture, which only I contemplate, for I hold the evil of the day to be sufficient without anticipating. After despatching my short letter and having finished my business I proceeded to Saharumpore, where I found my wife and child in high health with her parents—a venerable old couple. We returned home the beginning of November, and here we have remained without any change. It is certainly the most charming climate in the world, and its merits have *at last* been acknowledged by Government! who have ordered Barracks to be erected for convalescent European soldiers and Bungalows for sick and convalescent officers and sanctioned a regular establishment of a commandant and staff. This will make our situation more lively and gay, which was all it wanted to render it most enviable. This, I fancy, is all owing to Metcalfe's representations: he spent last hot season with us. To give you some idea of the place I shall endeavour to get a rough panorama sketch of the Dhoon taken from the top of our Castle at Deyrah. A rough pencil sketch would give you some idea of the nature of the country, and a leaf out of my report would give you an idea of the natures, manners and customs of these interesting high-

* Somerset House, near Coleraine, Derry.

landers! So you see, I am ready to meet your proposals with ardour, and in return for the hopes you hold out to me of the pictures of my revered parents to send you more than you requested for your cabinet collection. And I must tell you seriously that in making this offer I am not bragging, for I have already commenced a collection of birds and snakes for you which I think you will prize if they reach you safe. They are cured by our little native doctor, a boy brought up in my own school at Deyrah and taught to cure birds, &c., by my Adjutant, who has lately returned from England and has a taste and inclination that way. So you see you are likely to be gratified without any over-exertion of Jeanette, or myself, or our patience or perseverance!

"9th January, 1828. Press of business induced me to lay down my pen—and you know the family failing—once relinquished it is difficult to resume. Since laying down my pen, circumstances have occurred which threaten some alteration in our plans for next hot weather. First I got a letter from Colonel Stevenson—an old friend—apprizing me of Lord Combermere's intention of passing the coming hot season at Mussoorie*, and *on my Potato garden!* on account of the fine climate—giving me a hint that I might hear more of it. This was a bore—but little men must give way! I sent a full report of the localities to my friend S.——, who is Qr.-Master-General, at the same time putting my house at the disposal of his Lordship. Before my reply could have gone half-way I had a letter from Turner Macan, Mrs. Richardson's brother, who is Persian Interpreter and Secretary, asking me

* Now known as Mussuri.

without reserve: 'Will you allow Lord Combermere to occupy your house at Mussoorie in which Metcalfe spent the last hot season? His movements towards your quarter will be finally determined by your reply.'

"It was fortunate I had made the offer in the first instance with a good grace as I could not have avoided letting him have it!—Besides being C.-in-C. and a great man, an overland despatch from Bombay reports the death of Mr. Canning—which from my soul I hope is untrue—and goes on to add among other changes that Lord Combermere is to be Lord.-Lieut. of Ireland. Indeed Macan mentions it, but says it requires confirmation. This circumstance makes me anxious to have it in my power to show him attention. I want nothing for myself, but who knows what might turn up? and what opportunities of serving some of my friends might not arise on some future occasion from his recollecting the name of Young in consequence of attention to his comforts here, and a word from our worthy friend, Sir Charles Metcalfe, on his way through Calcutta to the Vice-Royalty! But, enough of castle building. I told Macan to assure his Lordship that the house was at his service, and his occupying it would not put us to any inconvenience, being already so well housed at Deyrah as almost to render a change in the hot weather superfluous! 'Angels and Ministers of grace defend us!'

"I had just got so far when in came the post with a large packet in Barbara's handwriting, franked 'Secretary of State's Office.' There were many other letters, public and private, but all were put aside, and you may guess with what delight we proceeded to open the packet and discovered the affectionate letters from Barbara, Susan and John, with the beautiful New Year gift from Barbara to Jenny. After perusing them we proceeded to look at the others—and oh! sad intelligence! we saw by the mourning paper that the death of Mr. Canning was confirmed.

"It is a melancholy occurrence—and seems to have thrown a gloom over England. We have not for ages had so popular a Minister: to him every liberal-minded man looked for the salvation of Ireland; with him our hopes have vanished! When can we expect to find so good a man, so firm a statesman, possessing his transcendent talents? I really never before felt so much the loss of any public character—but it is the will of Heaven. I fear poor Ireland is destined to suffer another age of mismanagement, and in the pangs of despair to gnaw her own vitals! I shall close this letter—the thread of my discourse is broken.

"Ever your affectionate Brother,

"F. Young."

Of those who are mentioned in this letter, Sir C. Metcalfe, Mr. Canning and Lord Combermere, are characters in history. The only private individual who needs a passing note is "Susan," who wrote one of the home-letters. She was not a Young, but a cousin, who always lived with my Aunt Barbara. We must feel highly-honoured to remember that she was a Miss Gage, of Rathlin! Rathlin is a rocky island off Bally Castle and has always been in the possession of a Gage from time immemorial. Indeed, a very learned and much-honoured old friend of mine, an antiquarian who loved ancient traditions and Celtic lore, once said to me laughingly: "If you have a Gage of Rathlin in your ancestry you can hark back to Cuchulainn."

Consequently it *has* happened that, when conversing with anyone who suffered from aggressive pride of birth, a little mocking devil from the north has impelled me to say: "*Our* family goes back to 400 B.C." Unfortunately the modern successors to the ancient line have not been millionaires. A rocky coast without a good harbour, however nice it may all be when you once get inside, is a difficult place of residence unless you can command all the modern adjuncts of transit to carry you to and from the mainland. I am afraid it is too true that in this present civilized age the reigning monarch has been obliged to abdicate. The island is still his but his family lives on the mainland.

Now there comes a long pause, and in the interval between the letters of December, 1829, and that of October, 1835, the little family of three daughters had become important members of the community!

"Landour, October, 1835.

"MY DEAREST BARBARA,

"Your letter written from Somerset, March 29th, 1834, reached me only a few days ago. It must have made a long voyage round the Cape, though you intended it to come via Malta and the Red Sea. Though of old date, it was a delightful letter, as all your letters are, and conveyed to us great pleasure and happiness. We are truly sorry to hear an unfavourable account of Miss Colgrave's school, for you will observe from my last letter I intended to have committed our three girls, Kate, Susan and Mary, to her care. But as you hint there is a possibility of you and Susan taking a larger house, so as to enable you to receive the three little adventurers we are about to part with, I do not hesitate to say if that plan can be carried into effect, and you can add a highly accomplished governess, capable of instructing the children in French, music and drawing, I need not say we should both feel more confident and easier in mind than under any other circumstances.

"The Castle I have built in my imagination is that the house selected be Tarnamoney, if it would answer and be sufficiently large to contain you all. If not, you can no doubt get some comfortable place that will do so, and the nearer Somerset the better! I should prefer a house in the country with a garden and a few acres, to one in Coleraine. There is no time to be lost. We all leave this place for Deyrah on the 10th inst., and, on the 20th March for the Ghat (embarking place) on the Ganges, three stages from Meerut, where we have boats ready to remove the three children and their Governess, Miss Philp, who accompanies them to Calcutta—and if it can be managed all the way to Coleraine. At Calcutta they will join our kind friend, Mrs. Dunlop, in the same ship with whom they will sail for London, and from whom you will probably have the first intimation of their arrival. When you wrote, Tom and Hatton had gone to the Continent to bring home his sister, Mrs. Layard, and you had taken up your abode at Somerset. I trust you had a prosperous journey. I am glad to hear the wine I sent John turned out to be good. I hope the Box of Birds which was dispatched from Calcutta shortly after Colonel Roberts sailed, reached Somerset safe. If I recollect right I put up some feather tippets that I think you would admire. I believe Jeanette intends sending some more of the same kind with the children: also the necklace she is preparing to send you she tells me to say if the hair is not neatly put in, which she doubts the capability of the Delhi workmen accomplishing, you can have it done over again at home.

"I hope you saw my friend, Pat Roberts. He and I were chums as Subs in the same Regiment for many a year. He was the Adjutant and I the Adjutant Quarter-Master for a long time. He will be able to tell you many an anecdote of the days of our youth. He is expected out to this country again immediately. Did you see his wife? She is said to be a very amiable and accomplished woman. Pat will be able to tell you all about Jeanette, as he knew her before we were married, and afterwards he stayed with us for some time in the Hills, when he was very unwell, previous to his marriage to his present wife. He is a very amusing companion and if he is in good health will give you many a hearty laugh!

"I met with a young man some days ago who brought a letter of introduction, Lt. Murray, an Englishman by birth but who has been much in Ireland, particularly at Culdaff. He told me his father married a Miss Young of Culdaff and that Brooke Young (General Young of the R.H.A.) was his Uncle. We have here young Staples, son of the Rector of Moville, where I was born. He showed me the picture of the house and grounds and I really recollected the place or fancied I did, though it is long and many a year since. . . . By the bye Hatton and Tom will have returned with his sister, Mrs. Layard, whom I think I recollect seeing in London at Sir Thomas Troubridge's when I was coming out to this country—a Cadet—a regular Johnny Raw from the Bogs. . . .

"Your affectionate Brother,
"F. Young."

This letter, as I foretold, re-introduces his early friend, Pat Roberts, and the interest round this memory culminates in the proud fact that his son was named Frederick after his godfather, Frederick Young, and became in due time the great soldier, the Empire's pride, and beloved by all who knew him, Field Marshal Lord Frederick Roberts, V.C., etc., etc., but known to the British Army as "Bobs." Of all he did and would have done a coming generation will more freely judge. I do not claim for him the gift of prophecy, but he had no doubt a power of prevision, and we should never forget that long before the stirring days of 1914 he selected and proclaimed the coming military genius of the century in a French officer named:

FOCH!

Talking of prophecies reminds me how, in the horrors of the Great War, when everyone was feeling out for words of comfort, encouragement and hope, many minds turned to the old prophetic writings of the Old Testament and built up *each one his own theory*, for there is much truth in the saying so fully proved at that time: "The Devil can quote scripture for his purpose." One passage hidden away among the many discussed chapters always reminded me of Fred Roberts:

> "If the people of the land take a man from among them and set him for their watchman: if when he seeth the sword come upon the land he blow the trumpet and warn the people, then whosoever heareth the sound of the trumpet and taketh not warning, if the sword come and take him away his blood shall be upon his own head. He heard the sound of the trumpet and took not warning, *whereas if he had taken warning he should have delivered his soul*."

The Mrs. Layard who was Tom Richardson's sister and whom my Father met as Miss Richardson at Sir Thomas Troubridge's in 1801 was the aunt of the well-known explorer of Nineveh, historian, and public servant of the State, who died in 1886 leaving a great record. He was born in 1817 and spent his boyhood in Italy. At 16 he was brought to London to study law, and it is more than probable that he formed one of the party of travellers to whom my Father refers.

There is no record of the final arrangements for the three elder children, but we know that they lived at Somerset for many years. Aunt Richardson's youngest daughter was the same age as my eldest sister, Kate, and their education was carried out together.

All this time the little motherless girl of whom I have spoken, who had been sent home to Ireland in 1814, was growing into a clever and accomplished woman, but alas! she was very feeble in physical health. She suffered from a spinal complaint and needed great care. She lived in Coleraine not far from Somerset, almost next door to her doctor, whose family was devoted to her. She had her own servants and establishment and was known as Miss Mary Dhoon. Of her wonderful personality, her attainments, and her many friends, I will speak further on. She passed across the stage in the days of my youth like a living fairy-story! and I never knew more of her than I have related in these reminiscences.

Aunt Hatton had married her cousin, Tom Richardson, of Somerset House, Coleraine. He was a clergyman but Somerset was his own property—a fine large property too—including a beautiful salmon-leap on the River Bann just across the broad road opposite his own gate. On the other side of the river was Mount Sandy where, at the top of its beautifully-wooded slopes, was an old Roman encampment. The

Richardsons had a large family of their own, older than the little ones now entrusted to them. Of course, I do not remember the departure of my sisters from the Dun. I was then the baby of the family, but when I was one year and four months old my nose was put out of joint by the arrival of a son and heir! He was called Charles Frederick after his Father and after a very notable man of the day, Sir Charles Metcalfe, who was his godfather and whose gold watch is still in the possession of one of my dear granddaughters. My brother Charles was succeeded in due time by two little sisters. In 1839 we four children, Louisa, Charles, Hatton and Marion, also went home to Ireland, but with us came our Mother.

This period from 1837 to 1840 is the time when my memory enters its deep and lasting record. I was an intelligent part of the scenes I recall. Many pictures of a sunny childhood—indeed babyhood—still linger round that beautiful valley, for I was just five years old when I left it. A cynical reader may say with a smile: "How ridiculous." But the accuracy of my statement was once thoroughly tested. The first time I re-visited the Dun was in my 42nd year. On that occasion my husband was the cynic. He challenged my confident memories and said it was quite impossible to retain such clear pictures of the first four or five years of a so-distant childhood. Naturally the valley was now a military cantonment, built over and deformed by civilization. A young Gurkha directed us to the house that had been built by Young Sahib. I refused to recognize it! "No," I said; "there was a large porch with a balcony over the front entrance."

We had a heated argument. My husband contended that a resident who belonged to the Regiment should know best.

So, arguing, we continued to walk round the house and my positive description was confirmed! Recent occupants, a banker or some business-firm, had used the back of the house for public entry. On arriving at the other side facing the snows my heart leapt to see what I had never forgotten! Elated by my victory, standing on the ground that had been trodden by my little feet so many years ago, I demanded paper and pencil. Before we entered the door I had sketched the position of the stairs and the plan of the rooms on the upper story—the verandah towards the parade-ground, where as children we used to play, and of which the minute details were reproduced by that loving glance into the past, even to the baskets of Benares toys and the swing with its gay green and red wooden rails. At one end were steps leading to the large bathroom where our ablutions were performed, and where (according to my hazy recollections) we had made naughty raids to *play with water*, that game all children love! I did not forget the drawing-room nor the ante-room leading from it to the other side looking towards the snow mountains. Empty and unfurnished as they were then I could replace the writing-table with the picture of Mazeppa on the wall above it. I can see them now, those dream-things of old days! And then—the great arch leading to my beloved balcony! I had not made one mistake. Even now in my 87th year, if a fairy-carpet were at my feet and I could fly "large lengths of miles" and stand there on a clear, starlit night, for one dear moment I would be a child again!

The reason why that balcony was so important to me was an incident that occurred in my fourth year. It is a memory far more vivid than many a more recent occurrence. My Father held me in his arms, and looking over the snowy mountains to the North he

HOUSE AT DEHRA DUN

[face p. 84

traced the Great Bear and the Polar Star—drawing the outlines with his pointing finger. The memory has been there from that day to this, when I have watched the revolving picture of that unchanging scene from different latitudes, in many different moods.

Of course the picture of the old house that used to hang in Father's study helped my memory with regard to the outward aspect, but it could give me no clue to the inner details.

CHAPTER VII

Early Experiences

> "There are vacancies which only Silence may dare to inhabit, which yet, to those whose very own they are give out a flooding of music all life long."

Of course in this period of my active memory one gracious figure is the presiding genius, but that sacred subject has always been locked away and never has the key been given to anyone so freely as now. So it remains "Sacred and pure of all words said," though through the next twelve years it remained the star of my life, the source of all my keenest joys and the fountain-head of all the best I ever knew. The echoes that bring that past back to me are *the secrets of little voices in beautiful Nature that never change or die*; the scent of fir trees in the sunshine; the smell of the wild white roses; the sound of running-water lapping on stones. And then also the measured tread of horse-hooves on a dry road in the dark. This comes to me like the refrain of music in the dreaming ears of a little child, curled up in the dearest and sweetest of shelters, never to be found again on this side of Paradise! But on this personal phase I am not going to dwell. In no way do I wish to write my own biography. The difficulty that occurs is this: writing from memory as I am, I cannot quite leave out the person who remembers! Lord Byron has truly said: "The subject on which a man is most eloquent is himself." Perhaps this applies even more to a woman! But in writing these memories I want to keep myself as looking on, standing outside, as it were, and recording what I have seen in old and vanished times. The world then bore a very different aspect, many features of which will never return. Its records may be interesting. No doubt little personal bits may slip in here and there in connection with the places and facts I draw into my narrative, but I will only consciously indulge in these divergencies when my life-story itself justifies me. But no doubt I have shared and taken my part in some remarkable historical and interesting events that are well worth recording.

In 1839 I was only five. My brother Charlie, three-and-a-half; Hatton, two; and the baby Marion, just arrived. I felt much older than the children; as companions they hardly counted, except Charlie, when he rode to the Parade-ground and was treated like a "Lord Sahib" and I was proud to ride beside him. Otherwise in all my daily memories I had one companion. I remember the morning walk to the garden between the wild rose hedges that sometimes overslipped their bounds and, climbing up the high trees, were carried on the light breezes from bough to bough, forming a natural pergola over the path. Here in the garden the finest carrots were drawn from the ground, washed in the running stream that makes music in all Indian gardens, and finally taken to gentle, expectant "Hector" and his stable-companions.

Then when the weather became too hot, we all moved up to the house on Landour. My fragmentary pictures of this time are probably quite different to the scenes of the present day when "prams" and "bikes" have done away with the picturesque conveyances of old. Of course the pony is always with us, and magic memory brings back little childish facts as if my eyes could still behold them, but so long as there are children and ponies these will be familiar to all, in all times. But I may speak of my little canvas palanquin—it was called a *doolie.* It was swung on a long pole and carried by bearers who sang as they swiftly moved, and by my side ran one more gorgeously apparelled than the rest. But he never joined in the singing. The foremost bearer improvised and the others caught up his words, but they all had the same refrain :

> " Humph, humph bearer,
> Juldi chullo bearer ;
> Mem barra hulka,
> Sahib burro dhari,
> Humph, humph bearer,
> Kubardarie bearer."

I used to know many of these ditties. The third and fourth lines nearly always varied to suit the occupant or the occasion, but they never forgot the anticipation of their journey's end when *dhal* and *chapatties* would be waiting to fill their " Little Marys " !

Probably not one tourist in a hundred now hears this once-familiar melody.

This procession used to take me to school and dancing-classes. In the rainy season it was covered by a square frame of wood with red cloth and curtains lined with wax cloth. I never smell wax cloth—such as we pack with—but it brings back the memory of the loud patter of tropical rain on my unsteady roof, and the joy I used to feel when I left my *doolie* in the verandah and was in safe shelter once more. I used to be frightened in these storms, but I never confessed it to anyone.

I remember one journey in my small conveyance on a clear, warm night under the stars, for I was taken to a grown-up fancy-dress ball as a tiny flower-girl with a basket of little bouquets on my arm. I recall a funny little incident that has often made me smile. An officer in full highland-dress carried my basket and lifted me up to sit on a stool beside him. His bare knees looked so funny under his tartan skirt that I put out a tiny hand and touched them to see if they were real. And I wondered why everyone laughed!

Then the great kaleidescope was shaken and the scene changed.

The dear Father was no longer there and we—my mother and the "children" and I—in a strange and novel isolation, were floating down the Ganges River!

This remains in my mind as a brilliant series of pictures might, and it is a record of a vanished experience that civilization and its needs have quite wiped out. I am here writing of 1839–40, and because it is a thing of the past and will never again be the familiar experience of the Englishwoman in India, I could wish I had a more artistic touch to bring before you all that I recall.

At that season of the year the great, swift stream had fallen low: skilled boatmen, our pilots, had to follow the right channel as the floods of last year had marked it out, for it changes with every rainy season. A desert of water lay around our large fleet of boats; sometimes a far-off green line marked the boundary of our isolated world. Rising above this plain of sparkling water there were mounds, and crinkled flats, and islands of sand on which strange, long-legged water-fowl paced in dignified slowness, as if asserting their monarchy over the shifting kingdom where they trod! Sometimes we would pass a twisted and tortured tree that had been ruthlessly torn up by its roots in full flood, sometimes the upturned keel of a wrecked boat: and sometimes, on rising ground against the bright sky-line, a temple-dome would appear half-hidden in a grove of trees.

At sundown we would always anchor for the night by some firm bank, near a native village generally, where the Bazaar could replenish stores; and here a varied panorama was created as if for our especial delight.

Every boat of the many that followed us would disgorge its load of our attendant servants. Scores of fires would be lit on the shore at the regulation-distance from each other, so that Hindus and Mohammedans might cook their dinners apart without fear of contamination.

The murmur of voices, the glare of the wood-fires under the moving veil of smoke, the ceaseless stir of the dark figures passing to and fro, is like a transformation-scene that rises before me now if I close my eyes and "remember"!

I do not recall much about leaving the *Budgerow* (as our floating home was called), but I think that we must have done so sometimes, because of an involuntary memory that once rose up from some hidden corner of its own accord! When reading Tennyson's *Palace of Art*, I came to the picture:

> "A tract of sand
> And someone pacing there alone
> Who paced for ever in a glimmering land
> Lit by a low large moon."

And suddenly there rose before my mental vision a picture painted in that wonderful gallery where we collect the shadows of our early years—and there they lie behind Time's curtain until some magic touch draws it aside and we see what has been! In one pulse-beat I was back again on a firm, white sandbank on a wide stream, lying in dim light, with the impression of a solitary great bird's claws on its smooth surface.

Now more matured thoughts cluster about that deserted highway. At that far-away time it was traversed by men and women like ourselves in every variety of life's phases, grave and gay. Fancy fills the vanished stage with shadowy forms that played their part in tragedies and comedies of long ago: and some of their reminiscences—like Bishop Heber's—still keep alight a lamp of remembrance.

Occasionally near our halting-place human habitations declared themselves and the outline of a military cantonment stood out against the gorgeous colouring of sunset-skies. Then always visitors would come and, plenty of *dhallies* for the Mem Sahib. Eighty years ago these were symbolic of the hospitality that never failed to greet the stranger in British India, but I fear few strangers are so greeted now. The *dhally* (called *dolly*) is a flat, covered tray of basket-work filled in pyramid-shape with fruits and vegetables cunningly and picturesquely arranged. In the cold weather they often included a delicacy unknown in civilised countries, so far as I have visited them. It consisted of a box of preserved grapes from Kashmir or it may be from Afghanistan. These appeared green and fresh, as when first gathered, and tasted most delicious. I do not think the secret has ever been divulged to the western world, and I wonder why, for in spite of all changes there are still some greedy people left! Each berry is taken off the bunch and lies separately in a bed of fresh, white cotton-wool. The grape is seedless. Not very long ago the head-gardener at Wisley looked at me with doubt when he showed us some vines on which they were trying to produce seedless grapes and I remarked "I have tasted them grown in Kashmir."

When we had anchored or *lagowed* near a cantonment we could hear in the silent, star-spangled night the fifes and drums of the "tatoo" calling absent soldiers back to barracks, and then, after silence, the echoes of the "Last Post" trembled on the air. The Last Post! Is there any music in the world that has such power to stir the bitter-sweet of old memories in a British heart?

How long it took us to accomplish our journey to Calcutta I cannot say. Dates do not linger in my mind. I think it must have been counted by months. We arrived in Calcutta in time for the season of sailing-ships that took the English home. That voyage also took months to accomplish, and is another experience blotted out by the racing pace of present-day travel.

I must pause here a moment to lay emphasis on that term "sailing-ship," and ask you to realize that these great vessels with their precious human freight were at the mercy of winds and waves, with no more defence against the tremendous powers of Nature than the brains of skilful navigators and the presence of mind and wonderful manipulation of ropes and canvas and fragile gear by strong fingers—the dauntless courage and indomitable will-power of sturdy British sailors. All honour to them; Hearts of Oak while there is land and sea!

I am so glad to remember "The Earl of Hardwick" and the time spent in her wooden walls. I recall her as a child might recall a visit to a country-house filled with guests: but naturally she had her characteristics. First of all there was the start from the Calcutta Harbour in the dark night and out to sea in the Captain's own boat. (I am so sorry I have forgotten the

Captain's name—I lovėd him dearly. I remember the first officer's name was Truscott, and I did not love him nearly as well.) I have a distinct feeling of going alongside the great black hull and being lifted miles up in the air until my little feet were firmly planted on the deck! Even at that early age I distinctly recognized that our journey in the Captain's boat was a particular privilege, which I shared with my Mother. "The children," the nurse and servants had preceded us long before; but then and throughout the voyage I felt myself rather a superior person.

No doubt my Mother's charming personality gained her much distinguished attention, and as I was always by her side I unconsciously claimed a share. I suppose there must have been some storms at sea during the long voyage, but they left no impression on me. That "The Earl of Hardwick" did occasionally roll in her gait I know by the story that became a nursery-joke in after-times that plump Baby Marion had rolled out of her cabin across the saloon and had been picked up by the ship's steward who thought it was a clothes-bag dislodged by the motion of the ship! Calm, lovely days I do remember, and children's parties given by my dear Captain—games, laughter and good cheer.

I have never sailed since or steamed across the great ocean and looked up past masts and rigging to the blue sky without remembering my first theological puzzle! One day the sailors caught a shark, and the great creature was laid out on the deck for us to walk round and survey with proper awe and wonder. Going to the church service on deck the following Sunday, sitting beside my Mother with the book in my hand (that I could not read!), but pretending to be grown up as all children do, I was arrested by hearing these words:

"When Thou hadst overcome the sharpness of death Thou didst open the Kingdom of Heaven to all believers."

I thought the man said "*the sharkness of death.*" I was still vividly impressed by the slain monster I had seen on the deck and at once I looked up to Heaven—as children's geography places it—and watched between the gently rocking masts and ropes for something to happen! But the serene blue gave no sign. Yet, *if it was written, it must be true.* I looked round—no one was casting expectant glances at the sky! What *did* it mean? "Thou didst open the Kingdom of Heaven to all believers." Certainly the shark had been overcome. Then the only way to explain it was *there were no believers.* Ah! that was it! Of course if they had believed they would have expected it, and of the whole assembly not one looked expectant. That was my first theological puzzle—the answer contented me!

Of course we touched at St. Helena; and here I have a curious vision. I do not know if it is a solid memory that anyone can confirm. I have never, to the best of my belief, constructed it on anything since seen, but I *still see it*—two willow-trees above Napoleon's grave and in *the space outlined by their branches* the silhouette of the great soldier in his recognized attitude! It was the work of Nature, not of Art, so it must have been short-lived; for branches grow and their forms alter every year. That is all I remember of St. Helena.

The Cape of Good Hope leaves a memory not much more distinct. It was not of grapes (it was the wrong season, I suppose), but what I *think* I remember is—beautiful, big sheep with snow-white, large tails that were kept out of the dust by a little sort of car-

support. The two things are very visionary as if I had seen them in sleep, and quite different from the other vivid things which I can record with confidence.

As we drew near to English shores there was much talking and excitement among the passengers, and everyone seemed to be thinking of some formidable obstacle that must be encountered. Its name was frequently mentioned. It was the *Custom House.* Of course in me it only roused wonder, for I could not help noticing that preparations for meeting this foe were carried out in mysterious whispers!

In Calcutta we had found everything from home awaiting us which we required for landing, and my great respect was given to the pelisse and tippet which were intended for my first British toilette! It was made of fine, soft, fawn-coloured cloth with a wadded lining of pale blue satin; and finally it was destined to become acquainted with mystery and the armour necessary to stay that dawning monster, the "*Custom House!*" My Mother knew that to me her will was law and that I would sooner die than displease her. So I was admitted into the council of war. It was carefully explained to me that all beautiful work in gold and silver would be looked at and, if not made in England, would be broken up, so that it was necessary to hide things, and that was why everyone had secrets. All the boxes would be opened and examined when you went through the Custom House. This was simple enough to understand. I grasped the fact that the pale blue lining of my cape and pelisse carried more jewellery than my small person bore at any other period of my history.*

* This is not strictly true. Many years after this I was cast for the part of Lalla Rookh in an amateur production of tableaux at Murree, at the house of the chief commissioner. All the ladies adorned me in their best jewels and I wore the celebrated gold scarf of Dighton Probyn's full-dress uniform. Before I went on the stage I was estimated to be worth a large sum, and the giants

Fortunately my wadded garment passed through this trial in safety, but it was not capable of shielding me from a personal calamity that filled my eyes with tears and my heart with a painful fury. I saw before my eyes the christening cup my grandmother had given me smashed ruthlessly into a shapeless mass. It was *Indian silver work*. I know nothing of laws and regulations of those days, I can only vouch for the barbaric fact!

I could give more details of this entrance to our native land, but, recognizing now that we were undoubtedly *smugglers*, I refrain from inculpating a larger body of transgressors!

of old, brave heroes of the Frontier, bearing names that the world has known, Peter Lumsden and Sam Brown, and many others dead now—only living in hearts and in the Empire's history—made their laughing plots to carry me off as I stood. Ah! It was good to be alive in those days of youth and sunshine.

CHAPTER VIII

On a Northern Coast

> "Folk say, a wizard to a northern King
> At Xmastide such wondrous things did show
> That through one window men beheld the spring
> And through another saw the summer glow
> And through a third the fruitful vines agrow
> While still, unheard, but in its wonted way
> Piped the drear wind of that December's day.
> So with this Earthly Paradise it is
> If ye will read aright, and pardon me
> Who strive to build a shadowy isle of bliss
> Midmost the beating of the steely sea
> Where tossed about all hearts of men must be."
>
> *William Morris.*

Of course after landing we passed through London and little bits of the transit are still alive to me!

I heard Braham sing *The Bay of Biscay*.

I saw a fairy-play called *Robin Goodfellow* (for where my Mother went I went). Driving through the streets after shopping I remember Baby Marion throwing her new toy out of the carriage-window. I can see it clearly now, a gaily-dressed jester with jingling cap and bells. My mental mirror must have been extra sensitive at the moment, and then I think it had a kind of collapse after all this excitement. I have no remembrance whatever of crossing the Irish Channel—or of the arrival in the Old Country—or of our first meeting with the elder children—or of any domestic matter!

In the first few months all personalities—except the One—were obliterated. I was only conscious really of the beautiful world that surrounded me; of its wild and absorbing charm and the strange-shaped rocks that came and went in the ever-changing field of water—and that water, the sea, never the same, as vivid in its calm as in its storm. On quiet, sunny days there were the deep green pools with the mysteries of life and movement in their clear depths and their seaweeds, and the mossy green covering the rocky slopes, to which the little shells were clinging. And those wide spaces of brilliant sand!—not like fresh-water sands that I remembered; and then the wild joy of racing buoyantly along the coast and flying on winged feet from one rock to another! it was an intoxication of living that knew no fear and gloried in daring leaps over hazardous places, as if my feet could not err.

Then by degrees "the children" and Nurse come into my picture and my ecstasies are shared. We used to walk up the steep hill, past the harbour under the headland to where, between the road and the rough coast, lay hills and valleys of sand with myriads of shells that looked all alike until gathered and then never one was like another! Here and there in the valleys were pools of water that took the proportion of lakes to our young eyes with the breeze playing their surface into waves and ripples, so that standing on a firm point we could look down and watch the moving water until it almost seemed as if *we* were moving on. Further in-shore there were wild stretches of yellow whin with their delicious scent on sunny days! How many memories rise that call up vain regrets—memories that lie in the secret, unspoken deeps. Oh! happy days of childhood, never can the thought of them come back without that sense of something far-away that is beyond our grasp. Even then I could hear that message on the sad sea-waves.

It was on that glorious shore that I first learned to hem. A sailor taught me. He was rigging a little boat for my brother, and he gave me the sails to hem. When I told him " I didn't know how," he taught me! For many a long day neither I, nor anyone else, noticed that I did not thread my needle in the orthodox way, but, as experts call it, needle'd my thread. However, I have used a good many needles since then, and *non sine gloria*, though perhaps I should not say so.

Other pictures of our early rambles belong to this date. One has the walk round O'Hara Castle which stood on what children might have called a " frowning precipice." It lay to the left of our curving street in that dear old seaside village of Portstewart; I never began that walk without a shiver of fear! It was my hidden secret. (In fact I was a great coward at heart, but I feared nothing more than that anyone should find it out.) Once a wall which supported a crumbling part of the lower portion of the hill had suddenly fallen down and killed—a pig! It looked as if it might fall again at any time, and then perhaps it would not be—a pig! We generally went this way after the winter-storms to search for treasure-trove washed up on the long stretch of sandy beach that lay beyond the Castle. Nurse was pleased if she found " silly things," like reels of cotton and bundles of tape; but we were content to see the great star-fish, and lovely big branches of seaweeds, both large and small: and then the shells, so big and beautiful! They were broken it is true (for rocks are hard) but their skeletons even were treasures, for we could see the lovely, polished, irridescent walls of the houses where the deep-sea fish lived. Then, when winter had passed away and spring-time came, there was Primrose Hill—a sunny slope rising almost from the sea and so thickly carpeted with the dear flowers that we hardly dared to tread, and had to pick basketfuls before we could sit down to rest. And their scent in the clear bright air! Tennyson said:

> "The smell of violets hidden in the green
> Poured back into my empty soul's frame
> The times when I remember to have been
> Joyful and free from blame."

Certainly it is the primrose that recalls my "joyous" days. I am afraid I was never "free from blame." From time immemorial my Irish nurse used to say: "Oh, Miss Loweysa, you're the Div'l's own child!"

Another picture of those days is—a real shipwreck! From the early afternoon of a dark, stormy day our faces were glued to the nursery window-pane, watching a doomed ship coming nearer and nearer, struggling against wind and tide which, beating with resistless force, were driving her into the rocky arms of our little bay. On the right hand there was a fairly sheltered little harbour which no doubt she was trying to gain, but we could see her halt and stagger against the fierce, opposing wind. It grew darker and darker, and only by the fitful light that gleamed and vanished and came again could we trace her progress over the mountainous waves that tossed her on the raging surface as she came nearer and nearer to destruction on that field of rocks which made our beautiful playground on calm days. It was quite dark when the end came. We could only distinguish moving lights; there was no sound but the roaring wind. They saved the crew, all but the cabin boy; they never found his body and said he had probably been swept off the wreck and carried out to sea. But Charlie and I firmly believed that he had done some heroic deed and would not leave his dying ship!

We lived in that dear home for four years. The figures of my elder sisters began to take form and develop characteristics: I and "the children" grew into more important personages. There were school-rooms and governesses and many escapades. These, however, are the personal reminiscences from which I wish to refrain, as this is only a sort of "marking time" on the march I mean to pursue. I will conclude this chapter by referring to one who early in life, when only thirty-seven, left a vacant place in the family—not only in our family but in her own little circle, for she had five children living when they suffered their irretrievable loss.

My Father mentioned her in a home-letter dated 1827: "We are blessed with a sweet babe" (then nine months old) "with whom no fault can be found in point of temper, health and appearance." (See p. 73.) Her children, grandchildren, and great-grand-children may find an interest here. She was called Catherine Mary after her two grandmothers, and at the time about which I am now writing she was in her seventeenth year. She was not beautiful but very charming and good to look at. Below the middle height, she had a graceful figure, fine eyes, and quantities of bright, sunny, brown hair, and a clear, healthy, fair complexion. Her forehead was broad and too high for beauty, but there were *brains inside.* She was well-educated, a good linguist in French and Italian, and her musical powers were as much natural as acquired. She had very pretty, dimpled hands, and her manipulation of the only instrument she played—the piano—was pleasing to watch. Any music she heard she could reproduce at once, but no training could give her a singing voice. Indeed, sad to relate, among the six daughters who grew up only the youngest had a voice that approached that of our Mother which, in speaking as well as in singing, was of unequalled sweetness. In Portstewart a large house at the inner end of the Crescent was inhabited by a retired officer named Major Babington. Portstewart was a very out-of-the-way spot. Not many gaieties flourished there, so an unexpected excitement and interest was created when it transpired that this elderly bachelor, who never went beyond the ordinary, hospitable routine of dinner-parties, contemplated giving a ball in honour of Miss Young's seventeenth birthday!

Naturally our nursery shared the sensation! I cannot recall any preliminaries, not even the dresses that Kate and my Mother wore on that important occasion; but I remember that, as we (*i.e.*, Nurse and "the children" and myself) lingered with longing looks outside the gate on the afternoon of the memorable day, Major Babington came out and, taking me by the hand, invited us to come in and see the decorations. Brilliant lights and glowing fires, for it was winter-time, flags, banners, and flowers galore—but one special corner of delight that in all my many festivities I have never seen repeated! In a small room off the ball-room the walls were like a green bower lit by coloured lamps and there were two chairs for resting a dancing couple; and with a pleased and meaning smile Major Babington pointed out to me the crowning beauty! Disguised among the leaves of the green wall there were bunches of *real luscious grapes, green and purple*, peeping out of their cool and pleasant shelter. What child could forget that decoration? This was the ball given to my sister Kate on her seventeenth birthday.

If there has been too much personality in this chapter of my story, it is because of my wish to leave a memorial of that dear spot where I spent the happiest period of all my life.

In the prologue I have expressed what I mean. It is

"A simple epitaph
To comrades passed away
Who rise to gild my evening grey
With phantoms of Youth's morning."

CHAPTER IX

Coming Home

Each man is many as a caravan
His straggling selves collect in tales like these.

In 1844 a change came in these childish surroundings. "*Papa was coming home!*" In those days we said "Papa" and "Mamma". Those who went before us had said "Father" or "honoured Father" or "honoured Mother", and in later days "Father" and "Mother" *minus* the "honoured" were reverted to. It was left for a later generation to adopt the abbreviations of "Daddy" and "Mummy", while the impertinent familiarities of "Governor" and other disrespectful titles came in later still, accompanied by other objectionable manners. They were the beginning of that unfortunate change in family-relationships which has produced results not altogether desirable! With us in 1844 "Papa" was on a pinnacle; we felt rather like elementary man thinking of unknown Deity! The whole household was thrilled, and so were the many relatives from whom he had been separated for 44 years. The rapid pace of life which is familiar to the present generation had not yet dawned, and the small event of a stranger's arrival, unnoticeable in these days, made then a stir among all the neighbours. India was distinct by six or seven months' journey. India had been the stage of most remarkable and dramatic events during the past half-century, and one who had played his part in the drama was coming among them to share their simple, ordinary, humdrum existence.

While we children had been playing on the sands of the sea-shore Time, with its measured tread, had brought promotion to my Father. He was now a colonel in the army, and having cherished and nurtured his dear regiment and his beautiful valley for *twenty-eight years—that is his proud record*—he had been sent as brigadier-general to command the district of Bundelkhand. I think during the five years of my Father's command everything went on smoothly; the task was not a strenuous one, and, so far as I can tell, was unmarked by any happenings worth recording. But these years, spent in hot, trying seasons so different to the beautiful climate he had been living in, had brought to him the consciousness that time was passing, and that he was not so young as he had been, and so at the expiration of his time of command his thoughts turned homewards and, "Papa was coming home!"

While "Mamma" and Kate are on their way to London to meet the returned wanderer I think I must revert to the relations outside our own family who were eagerly expecting him. Their names are familiar to us in those home-letters that cheered his happy exile in the Dehra Dun; and a few words on the subject here will serve as a link between the descendants of Frederick Young and his many connections in the North of Ireland where some cousins may still be found. But the quickly-passing generations have made most of them into "cousins" several times "removed"!

First of all comes my Aunt Richardson, my Father's eldest sister, Hatton. She and her husband, Tom Richardson of Somerset, had taken care of my elder sisters when they left the Dun in 1835. Her husband had died, and she lived with her daughters in Portstewart. Somerset *now* belonged to her son Henry, who had married a daughter of the Countess of Antrim, and I think they had gone abroad on their wedding-tour and were absent from Ireland. The daughters—four of them—were all highly educated: they had done the "grand tour," which was an essential part of fashionable education in that time: had been properly introduced into society; and bore the brand somewhat emphatically—as they were rather exceptional cases in this quiet society!

My aunt was a remarkably clever woman, landed in a very level line of prosperous country-life; her gifts and talents, which might have developed beyond high-water mark, never received the tidal influence to carry her along. They say that sometimes, after a lapse of generations, there is a recrudescence of notable traits, mental and bodily; and therefore, long after I have passed away, some of the little ones I know and love now—or the children who will follow them—may be very distinguished and remarkable, showing traits like those of the sister of their great-great-grandfather, Hatton Richardson, neé Young! She was a handsome woman, rather above middle height, with a somewhat brusque manner, but she could unbend to laughter and used to say amusing and witty things. To me personally she was always kind. She was a great gardener, and I loved to wander with her among her flowers and to help when she permitted. She lived in a house at the far end of the long village-street and—in a vivid picture that will always remain with me—I can see the far-away porch, and through the dark of a winter-evening a bright and shining light. Probably it is a Christmas-memory, for it is associated with warm wraps, and lantern light, and "party" anticipations. (Often, in those dear days when a child may wonder to its silent self, I used to look at the twinkling stars and think they might be lights in pleasant windows, and that the happy angels were always going to parties!) Her house was just across the road above the bathing-place—that spot of glorious memories—and hungry children rising from the sea-waves would run across to the house and blissfully devour thick slices of bread and butter, *Irish* butter! That is my embodiment of Aunt Richardson: the lighted porch; the bread and butter; and the gillyflowers in the garden. They are called "single stocks" now, but the scent is just the same as in my dream-garden of eighty years ago!

Her daughters were Kitty, Fanny, Barbara and Mary. All were different; Kitty, bright and merry, though dignified; Fanny, stately, soft and gentle; Barbara, handsome and vivacious; and Mary, a little gentle and near-sighted girl, much smaller and more retiring than her sisters. Kitty married Major Scott of Willsborough; Fanny married Captain Moore of Ballydivity; both were men of property in the North of Ireland. So long as I heard anything of them their families were not likely to be extinct, but other families were being drawn into the circle, and all are now lost to my sight! Barbara, some years after, married the Rev. Thomas Torrens, and their only son, John, is still in the same countryside, and occasionally still we exchange greetings. Mary never married but attained a placid old age. Barbara and Mary in their youth were the musical members of the family, quite famous for their singing of Italian duets. I never hear the long *duo* from *Norma* without the picture reviving in my mind of tall, dark-eyed Barbara and little, near-sighted Mary, standing behind their accompanist and going through the varied passage, from "Norma! Ah! Norma!" to "Si, finl al ore," with all its wonderful trills and flourishes. I always listened with wonder and amazement. At that time my musical appreciation was quite undeveloped, but I was divided as to who really deserved the laurels, and felt quite inclined to decide on our nursery-music as being of a more pleasing quality. It was certainly unusual! Little round-a-bout Marion, still a baby of four or five, was born like a bird with a natural music in her voice. Many who read this may remember that Aunt Marion could sing, but they will not know that at that early age she felt the necessity of musical expression, and had very cleverly improvised a piano on which she played her own accompaniment! The nursery tub of those days was just a square, tin tub of goodly size—about 3ft. by 3ft. and 1½ft. deep. It was used for the family every night and disengaged all day. So our fat and fair *prima donna*, with any assistance she could get, would drag it from its resting-place, set it up on edge, draw a stool up to it, and, with her strong little fingers hammering out a sort of muffled drum-accompaniment, would carol like a bird. She picked up any tune she heard and, fitting it to nursery-rhymes, would give us a miniature opera. I never remember Nurse or anyone telling her to stop. She did not know any consecutive rhymes, and her tunes too were mostly shreds and patches, but she would go on as solemnly and seriously as if she had been performing on the platform of some great hall. Latterly one performance used to turn us into *dancing dervishes*, even Nurse and her subordinate being unable to resist the infection! no Jazz of the present day can exercise a more powerful spell. It was the thing of *that* day and every one knew the words and the tune. The table was pushed aside, and Nurse and children and dolls—there were no teddy-bears then—whirled round in frantic energy, while Baby played the tin tub with all her might, marking time, as we all sang:

> "'Tis sweet on summer eve to roam
> A'down the river Tolka;
> But, oh! it is a sweeter thing
> By far to dance the Polka.
> Can't you dance the Polka?
> Won't you dance the Polka?
> The joys of earth are little worth
> Unless you dance the Polka!"

and the refrain was to what they called a heel-and-toe performance, which was our great delight. This is an unpardonable interlude and I must get back to business!

Our other aunt, Aunt Barbara, lived in Coleraine, a few miles from the sea, on the River Bann. We saw her very seldom but we all loved her; she was merry and fascinating; rumour said she had been very much sought after, but whether she preferred to be her own mistress, or whether the course of her true love had not run smooth, I do not know; but the fact remained that she and her cousin, Susan Gage of Rathlin, were evidently well-content to remain merry spinsters! On the rare occasions when we went to see her we all loved her; but still we felt—as children soon realize—that her household goods were household gods, and that, however high our spirits might be, we had to mind our manners and treat all her property with proper respect. She died rather suddenly, shortly after my Father's arrival, but I do not recall anything except the fact.

Then there was John Young, my Father's only surviving brother. He was rector of Tydavnet in Co. Monaghan, and had married a Miss Cromie, who was well-connected in the North; and they had two daughters and a son. The eldest daughter, Annie, was by far the handsomest of all my cousins. She had inherited the beautiful, refined face of her Father and grandfather, and was tall and very graceful. I remember that she was artistic, and I have a very clever caricature, done by her, of an old aunt of my Mother's, Mrs. Balfour Ogilivie, who was a famous *raconteuse*: she is speaking and emphasizing her story with spectacles in hand. Annie married Mr. Gervais of Cecil in Tyrone, and her granddaughter, married to Mr. Rhodes, is now owner of the place. Annie's own daughters are two maiden-ladies living in Bath.

Her sister Hatton never married, nor did her brother Gardiner, of whom I should like to say more. He was a most clever and amusing companion but wanting in ambition and energy. He took life's pleasures on the surface, was much loved by those who knew him, and I have always thought that, if he had been given a choice as to his career when a young man, his life would not have been so purposeless and trivial. However, he died unmarried, so the only cousins who could come in that line would be through Dorothy Rhodes (née Gervais) of Cecil: I do not think she has any children, up to date.

And then the wanderer, so much expected, arrived at last. There were flags, and rejoicings, and fireworks, and welcomes, and speeches, and a general stir in the calm life of Portstewart. The hotel was full and strange faces greeted us everywhere. Of course this change in the general routine made a great difference to me personally. It meant visits to country-houses, and parties, and dinners for the elders, which naturally resulted in some lonely hours for me. Then there was more nursery and schoolroom and systematic control, which gave rise to spasms of disobedience and revolt that added a zest to life! I remember that Charlie and I snatched old hats from the hall, and rushed out of the open hall-door, instead of gravely entering the schoolroom for which Nurse had prepared us. It was a lovely summer morning and we spent a heavenly time all by ourselves among the sand-dunes on the road to Portrush. There was no one at home whom we minded vexing, and we came back at sundown, happy and tired and probably hungry, and went to bed—*untroubled by the scoldings.*

This was the beginning of Father's two years of furlough and, though there is no brilliant historical event to record, I want to give you a picture of him at this time—not so much the impression of a child, but as advanced experience and knowledge of life enables me to see him. I want to throw this acquired side-light on this ordinary story.

Ireland in the North was a very quiet and almost sleepy corner of the world so far as society was concerned. He had left it on the verge of his fifteenth birthday. Of those who had been his best and dearest in youth many had passed away, and for those who remained to welcome his return, the experiences of life had been calm and prosperous with only ordinary thrills of births and deaths and marriages to break the monotony. He was like a glorious ship that had ridden on mighty waves and lived through battles and storms and suddenly found herself in a land-locked harbour with smaller craft that had only sailed on summer-seas! Of course he was fêted and made much of, and he had his dearest round him and knew once more the joys of his home-life. The milder pleasures, too, of the old sports in the old surroundings had their charm, but, regarded from this distance, we can now appreciate the fact that he must have been conscious of a strong contrast. If, at this distance of time, we try to put ourselves in his place, we realize that ties, such as those that had bound him for years, could not be suddenly brought to naught, and how, in his idleness, he must have heard the bugle call across the sea! For the country of his adoption was not at rest. And it must have affected him keenly at times that those moving in the society with which he mingled, though they showed him their kindly and enthusiastic appreciation, stood leagues aloof from him in their point of view, and gave two or three times more thought and interest to things of the day—*the new Penny Post for instance*—than they did to the important happenings in that far-away Empire beyond the seas, where men were laying down their lives for the honour of their land. I will illustrate what I mean. Very many years after this I went to a large "at home—music and dancing" at the house of a county magnate. My hostess was a very pleasant friend and neighbour and, standing near her shortly after my arrival, I said: "What terrible news this morning!" She stared at me in wide-eyed surprise. "What news?" It was only the "*Destruction of Colonel Hicks and his brave force on the way to rescue Gordon.*"

"Oh!" she said in a relieved tone, "I had not noticed. I don't know anyone there!"

Having been for so many years a well-known host the duties of hospitality were to my Father a second nature, and he quickly sought for means of returning all the festivities that he had attended.

He looked for and found a large house some few miles from the sea, near Coleraine. It was a very Irish house—which means that it had its drawbacks as well as its charms. The grounds were very pretty. The house stood on the banks of the River Bann.

The lawn sloped downwards to a stream, and across its stony course of bubbling water there was a thick plantation—the Paradise of our young days! There was a large garden, and orchard, and meadows, and arable land, dairy, stables, hay-loft, and pigs and grazing cattle. Oh! how large and grand it looked before our childish eyes. It was called "Ballysally." I saw it again many years after—the wand of enchantment no longer waved over it! But there was a fine kitchen and pantry, and a large dining-room most conveniently situated, a broad staircase and roomy landing, and an ideal drawing-room, with four long windows facing the lawn and showing the curve of the river and the beautifully-wooded suburbs of Coleraine. In this drawing-room there was the most beautiful fire-place I have ever seen in the British Isles. Indeed the only one that surpasses it, in my experience, is that glorious specimen of alabaster with its inner tint of rose that looks like a hidden flame, in the Gezirah Palace; it was adorned by that reckless Ibrahim Pasha when the beautiful Eugénie was his guest. In this old house of Ballysally the mantelpiece was of pure white marble: the shelf was supported by two full-length cupids, and on the centre slab between them was a basket of delicately-sculptured flowers. Those cupids were impressed, not only on my mind, but sometimes on the side of my head, being about my own height! For my sister Susy, with admirable sleight of hand, used to knock our heads together if, when standing round the winter fire, she thought I was talking too much and might inadvertently disclose some of her many secrets! Up the broad carriage-drive visitors came and went, and never was there a more courteous and popular entertainer. At the big dinner-parties he could not fail to recount at times the wondrous things he had seen and known in exploring that beautiful land, then an unknown country; they were marvels indeed to his untravelled listeners. Years afterwards I heard him tell this story. We were talking of travellers' tales. I think it was in connection with the French explorer in Africa who discovered the gorilla, and he laughed to think of the credulity of the stay-at-homes and of how often they swallowed a lie and would not believe a truth. He said that during his first furlough, in talking to some garden-lovers, fired by his beautiful memories, he had spoken of the wild white rose of the Himalayas that climbed, scenting the air, to the higher branches of tall fir trees and, blown by the breeze from one tree to another, made a canopy overhead. How they had laughed and pointed their fingers at him and called him "Baron Münchausen!" He had not defended himself, but the lurking imp of fun in him had prompted him to try another line. So he had said, "One day, riding through a jungle with dispatches, I saw a barrier across my path that I mistook at first for a fallen tree, but, as I was about to jump over it, I saw that it was a big snake that had just dined, and so I slashed at it with my sword and, the skin being cut, it split open—and up jumped a deer, horns and all, and ran away!" That *was* wonderful, and they had believed it! "Yes," he said, "whatever the snake might have done, *they* swallowed it—horns and all."

Just to add another touch of reality to the story of this time apart from its graver *significance* I will put in a childish escapade that lights up old memories. The back-stairs from the kitchen-apartment to the nursery recurs to my mind as the jovial scene of many naughty triumphs in which Charlie and I were chief actors. I had an early talent for mimicry of voices.

One of the outdoor men, a fine strong heavy Irishman (the other servants always called him the land-stewart) had a gruff voice which was my delight. I often used it to amuse myself. For instance, when Charlie was cautiously trying to climb the wall for some delicious apples that we called duck-apples, because they grew near the duck-pond, I used to say suddenly, "Miss Loweyser," and Charlie startled would fall, or drop his booty! It was a joyful moment. He boxed my ears when he could get at them. Our cook was called Nelly; she and William McLoghlin were great friends. Early every morning there was a special preparation of stir-about (or brochan) in a special saucepan waiting for an expected summons. Whether it was one of McLoghlin's perquisites or an extra favour I do not know. *My* business was to say "Nelly, is me brochan ready?" and then two fleet-legged miscreants would dash up the back-stairs and watch with delight over the banister to see the blushing Nelly emerge with her steaming bowl! We bubbled over with mirth as she retreated with a muttered "Div'l take them childer!"

CHAPTER X

How News from the Five Rivers Came Over the Sea: 1845

> "So let me sing of names remembered
> Because they, living not, can ne'er be dead
> Or long time take their memory away."

I want to keep the time at Ballysally free from personal and social details and to dwell on it in connection with my Father's individuality viewed from a broader standpoint.

We must not forget that when he landed in Ireland in the summer of 1884 he was on the eve of his 58th birthday. We know that in appearance, in energy and activity of mind and body, he seemed marvellously superior to the home-staying people of his generation; those long years of strenuous work had placed him, in experience of life and also in its demands, far in advance of them all; outwardly he was the untiring, courteous host at home, the popular guest abroad, universally loved by rich and poor. In spite of his bright and cheery ways, his laughter-loving nature, there was a second self that mere idleness would not content. He had been a man of action all his life, but it was an inherent quality in his nature, one that distinguished him in every phase of his life, that he did not "wear his heart upon his sleeve," or ever in word or deed advertize his inner self. I remember one act of his that could not be totally ignored, but no one ever arrived at details of the facts. It was not for want of asking!

I daresay even now some remain who cling to the old idea:

> "The Heathen in his blindness
> Bows down to wood and stone."

with its literal and misleading teaching. An Englishman once told me that, in conversing with an intelligent native of the so-called uneducated classes in India, he touched upon this missionary's idea. "No, no, Sahib," the man laughed; "I have a stone in my hut; I look at it when I worship, because it makes me concentrate my thought on the Power that made the universe, of which it is a part. Sometimes I place a flower there—it is my expression of gratitude for the beauty that is given to all." If this is a true description of a heathen I think we may conclude that they are all round us everywhere—in less spiritual guise. Who among us does not possess some treasure of remembrance that fixes our thoughts on something we love, often awaking the pain that is so akin to pleasure in certain minds? This is not digression but illustration. Just outside the gateway-entrance to Ballysally carriage-drive there is a hump in the road which indicates a bridge over the rippling stream that runs past the plantation I have spoken of: then the road rises rather steeply to where on the left hand is a little cluster of tree-shaded cottages. On a shelf in one of these cottages there used to be a *treasure of remembrance*—such as I mean—of so peculiar a nature that I think it should be recorded here. It made that cottage a sort of Mecca for the children of the "big house" as well as their poorer neighbours.

I have said that my Father at this age was a fine specimen of humanity as regards strength and activity. Walking in one of his fields which was divided by a high iron paling from the meadow where cattle grazed he was horrified by seeing a young bull in pursuit of a small boy. He somehow surmounted the paling—not before the poor child had had one toss in the air, but soon enough to prevent a repetition. A man entering the meadow from behind a hedge saw the struggle between man and beast, and came at the critical moment to my Father's help; they mastered the angry animal. The man when questioned said he "couldn't rightly say *how* the Colonel got into the meadow, or what happened; he had seen him walking quietly in the adjoining field just before." My Father's answer to inquisitive people was characteristic and final. He looked them straight in the face, lifted his hand, and said "*bus*," which is the Hindustani equivalent for "enough"; it was more final than many words! However, the end was that very gently he carried the boy home to his mother. We may rest assured that the best assistance was promptly summoned. It had been a near thing. From the wound in the head a little bit of protruding bone had been extracted and *that bit of bone* was the mother's *treasure of remembrance*. She never wearied of relating all the circumstances and her deep gratitude to the man who had saved her boy's life. That bone became a widely-known relic. As children we carried up many a basket of good things to the little convalescent with the bandaged head: always, blessings were invoked and the story told of the Colonel and his brave deed.

An essential memory of Ballysally must take its place here. It is nothing; and yet it is much, as collecting the threads of a narrative which has to be founded on so feeble a ground as a child's memory of great and unforgettable facts.

It was the time closely following the Cabul Retreat, one of the most bitter disasters that ever befell the

British army. To make that past history of its cause intelligible, I will, as in other cases, briefly tell the story here. One of those unfortunately familiar waves of peaceful assurance had swept over the calm minds of the British public and their rulers. Then, as in 1913, they had chosen "a watchman" who faithfully "blew the trumpet, but no man heeded," although the watchman was no other than the Duke of Wellington. The result was that in the northern parts of India only very small and inefficient forces were posted at distant points, under Colonel Sale and General Nott. Our faithful ally Runjeet Singh, chief in the Punjab, had died. Shah Shujah, deposed by Dost Mohammed, was restored to the Afghan throne. Dost Mohammed, surrendering his usurpation, was most leniently treated by the Indian Government, and this laxity—*never comprehended by eastern people*—had its usual lamentable effect. It gave encouragement to the disaffected and seditious leaders who preferred their own rule to ours. Of the resulting retreats, murders, assassination, and disastrous climax we need not tell more than what caused them. But —*we should not forget!* The memory of mistakes ought to be a useful tonic. Time with its cruel erasing touch wipes away much that ought to stand out in history. I do not suppose that even among educated people one in a thousand now could recall the name of "the last man"—the *one survivor* who reached Jellalabad. His picture was painted by a famous artist and for some years held the public interest. The name of that "last man" was Dr. Brydon.

I can recall many a tearful interview in the little dressing-room off my Mother's bedroom. I had never separated myself from her, and I was closer to her in her sorrows than her joys. How my dear

Father sympathized and comforted her in their mutual grief for sufferers leagues away from the British Isles, thinking each other's thoughts, as they read of the trials and pain and death that were breaking old friendships of past happy times (times when death and danger alike were unthought of) in that happy home they had shared for nearly twenty years!

The terrible retreat from Cabul had really taken place in January, 1842; but it was not until much later that distant rumours arrived at home; news did not travel as now, and I remember it was in our first winter at Ballysally (1843) that Lady Sale's journal, published after her return to England, came to hand, with all the authentic details of that great calamity. Nearly all the people mentioned there were well-known to my parents, and some were intimate acquaintances and friends. Of course it was then a story of the past, and the great perils were over for the survivors, but many familiar, often-mentioned names came into the sad story. I have now an old cross-stitch pattern on paper, such as every woman worked from in those days, and on it in my Mother's hand is written *Mrs. Hugh Boyd's pattern*, 1838, and it suggests her story in that dreadful time. Mrs. Hugh Boyd, shortly after the commencement of the retreat, was placed on a camel with her eldest boy, in what they called a *kajour*, a sort of basket-work pannier. This camel was unfortunately shot, so they removed her from the *kajour* and placed her on a small pony, while a mounted soldier, or servant, took the boy on the saddle before him. Almost immediately afterwards this poor man was shot and Mrs. Boyd saw her child carried out of her sight by the Afghan enemy! For long, weary months she had no reliable news of him, only conflicting rumours of a disquieting nature: eventually, I am glad to say, he was restored to her.

I only mention this one instance among many *far more appalling* to show how nearly the whole thing touched us, and the feelings aroused in the memories of both my Father and Mother.

All this time they were taking their part in the social life around them. In their close connection with the far-away tragedies, they painfully realized and sorrowed over the facts. To most other people amidst the passing events of the day which concerned them, these things that were so vividly real to my parents seemed only like far-away shadows of remote wars; they were wrapped round in a different atmosphere where, as a rule, nothing ever happened!

Then, as time went on, came fresh rumours of stirring events. A long-foreseen, but sagaciously-regarded and prepared-for, climax was approaching. It was the Sikh war. A certain number of India's most skilful and unflinching warriors were desperately bracing themselves for a hoped-for, and confidently relied-on conquest, which would drive the western invaders from the kingdoms where they were not wanted by these rebel-leaders. It was true that these invaders had pacified the country, and had established rightful rulers over aggressive and encroaching foes, and that to permit the return of the old order would involve the provinces in confusion and anarchy and a recrudescence of primitive barbarism. So that which the invaders had gained for the inhabitants of the land had to be maintained at all costs. A struggle was bound to come, but the dawning hopes for future progress must not be crushed by barbaric methods. The great problem was: how to meet the inevitable with strength and promptness, so as to give short rein to the conflict and minimize the cost in lives and substance, thus securing what diplomacy and peaceful effort had been unable to accomplish.

I am neither soldier nor diplomatist, I can only say: read Sir Charles Gough's *The Sikh and the Sikh Wars* and you will understand it all. On this little dial *my* needle points *back* to the old quarter. There were giants in those days. Their names were coming before the world to live in undying history, and my Father knew them all as friends and comrades—Hugh Gough, Robert Sale, Robert Dick, Pat Grant, Thackwell, Raleigh Gilbert, Sir Harry Smith, General Wheeler.

How eagerly the slow-coming tidings were looked for, and how they watched the increasing public interest, with which their own personal interests were so intimately blended! My Father looked eagerly forward, and remembered that he was still an active participator in the service of his country; and my Mother, with her full-hearted friendships and respondent sympathy in public questions, now as always shared his feelings.

The first battles in that campaign were Mudki and Ferozeshah; one quickly followed on the other, and they covered the dates from the 18th to the 22nd of December, 1845. I leave all details, and pass on to the third battle which holds our more particular interest.

After the heart-breaking losses that prefaced our victory at Ferozeshah it was necessary to pause and concentrate our remaining and scattered forces. The Sikhs were not idle. Fresh stores of artillery were coming to them from Lahore and they were being reorganized by the arrival of large bodies of well-trained soldiers.

We had ordered troops to advance from distant

stations in the plains and in the hills towards Ludhiana, and it seemed to be the design of Sirdar Runjoor Singh to threaten Ludhiana and cut our line of communication.

Sir Harry Smith who, with a slight strengthening of his force had easily reduced and taken possession of Dhrumkote, was ordered to proceed to Ludhiana, relieve that place, and join up with the forces collecting there. He started on the 20th January, marching to Lugraon so as to *skirt round Runjoor Singh* and move past him into Ludhiana. We shall see presently that this intent was not carried out without considerable danger and a narrow escape from something much worse! Among the troops now ordered to assemble at Ludhiana were two of the three memorable battalions that my Father had raised in the Dehra Dun, after the Nepal campaign. Although in the interval the men had been freely and successfully employed on several occasions—as for instance in the taking of Fort Kunjah as far back as 1824, of which I have given the authentic and corroborated account —by some extraordinary process such as occasionally distinguishes the tardy workings of British Governments, these battalions of brave and loyal men had not as yet been enrolled as part of the *Indian regular army*, though so freely employed as such! Now they formed part of the force that was collecting to reinforce our army in the field. The long letter I am going to quote was written by Colonel John Fisher, on that occasion commanding my Father's own regiment, the Sirmur battalion of Gurkhas. Written by the intimate and valued friend through many years in the happy valley, this soldierly and attractive narrative would thrill any military reader and therefore we can imagine how it was read in that far-away Irish home. After Sir Harry Smith had "skirted round him" Runjoor Singh had fallen back from his position at Budhowal to Aliwal, on the banks of the Sutlej. Of what the historian calls the "affair of Budhowal" *there is no official record*, and therefore this letter of John Fisher's is of particular value. Also, we may take it that it emphasizes the value of that proverb the teaching of which is somewhat difficult to follow at times: "discretion is the better part of valour." Discretion in this instance was salvation, but we will let John Fisher tell his own simple story.

> "On the 21st, Sir Harry Smith made a forced march to Loodhiana,* but either from want of proper information as to the enemy's strength or from ignorance of the line of march, he went too near their position, was attacked on the march, and dreadfully pelted by their artillery, losing between three and four hundred men, without returning a shot (except a round from *our* guns), his orders being not to hazard an action, but to relieve Loodhiana and unite his force with ours. This was bad enough but he lost besides nearly the whole of the baggage of the force both public and private. Whilst the cannonade was going on, we (the Loodhiana troops) marched out to meet him and reached his column just before the pummelling was over, and a very miserable and distressing scene it was, for the men were dead beat from fatigue and thirst. It was not a pleasant reunion at all.
>
> "The whole force moved into Loodhiana and halted there the 22nd and 23rd. Sir Harry moved to Budhowal with his little army, the Sikhs having retired from it on the 22nd and taken up a position

* Now known as Ludhiana.

at Aliwal about 10 miles from Budhowal, on the banks of the Sutlej, and covering the fords. We were occupied at Budhowal in getting all ship-shape again after the unlucky mishap of the 21st, and of course great exertion was necessary to make the Force efficient after the loss of baggage and stores, but things soon began to assume a more cheerful aspect. The troops were all burning to avenge the insult—and make the Sikhs disgorge their plunder.

"On the 26th Wheeler's Brigade joined us with the 5th Cavalry and Body guard and six guns as well as the Shekawattie Brigade under Major Foster. On the 27th the Force was brigaded regularly, and for the attack of the next day we marched as follows: Guns 34, 10.9 pdr., 2 10in. Howitzer, 22 Horse Artillery 6 pdr.

"Cavalry: 16th Lancers, 1st, 3rd, 5th Cavalry Body Guard Horse 600. Hill Irregulars. Infantry 31st, 5th, 53rd Foot; 24th, 30th, 36th 48 N.I. Sirmoor Batt. 47 N.I. Batt. Shekawattie. Our Brigade was: 48 N.I. 50th Foot and Sirmoor Batt. under Brigadier Wheeler, and was ordered to be in the centre column of attack.

"On the morning of the 28th I arose at 3 o'clock, wrote my will, and some farewell letters. At gunfire we all took our places in the Brigades, and our little army marched towards the enemy's position across the open plain in separate columns of Brigades. We knew that many a gallant spirit would be laid low ere many hours passed away, but we all chatted and joked as we moved along, confident of victory at any rate, though we only numbered 5,000 Infantry, 3,000 Cavalry and 34 guns, principally 6 pounders! The enemy had 32,000 men and 67 guns in position almost all of larger calibre than ours. Fearful odds! About half past nine we came to the old bed of the Sutlej and saw the Sikh army drawn up in battle array glistening in the morning sun: their heavy bodies of cavalry masking their guns, and quietly awaiting our attack, whilst a conspicuous chief, on a white charger, now and then dashed along their front. We descended the bank to the level flat below—which, up to the enemy's position was a hard plain on which one might have played cricket—without a bush or a tree between the armies. The morning beautifully clear, and not a particle of dust as we drew up in line—the Infantry in Echelon of Brigades the Cavalry on the Flank—under Cureton. The Artillery in the intervals of Brigades and with the Cavalry. This was all done as if on the Meerut parade—and when all was ready about half past 10 the whole line advanced steadily towards the Front. The enemy's cavalry slowly drew off to the rear to unmask their guns, and when our line had got within about 800 yards, the ball opened with a discharge of all their heavy guns; the round shot came leaping across the flat like huge cricket balls distinctly visible to the eye as they bounded towards us—but dashing to atoms, nevertheless, every man and horse they hit. They went steadily on—heads and legs and arms flying—till within about 500 yards when our Artillery opened: but at first—had only the effect of making the enemy redouble their fire and it became so tremendous on our Brigades, that Wheeler promptly ordered his whole line of three Regiments to lie flat on their faces. Here we lay for 10 minutes, the Sikh guns thundering away, answered merrily by ours, and our two big Howitzers playing over our heads from the rear with shells. The balls actually hailed upon us in all shapes, round shot, shells, canister and grape, and the din was infernal! Wheeler at last found that the enemy began to hit our range so exactly that he ordered us to rise, and advance, and when we had got about 150 yards nearer to their guns he again made us lie flat. Just as I rose when we were ordered to advance, one of my poor fellows was hit by a round shot, which sent his head and shoulders close past me to the rear 10 or 12 yards—his cap flying some feet into the air and whirling round and round. We laid on our second hard couch for about 10 minutes more, when the fire of the Sikhs began to slacken and the word was passed. *Up and at them.* We gave *our old Deyrah Hurra!*—which was taken up by the rest of the Brigade—and went pell-mell at the entrenchment at the double. Within about 80 yards the Sikh Infantry hidden behind the entrenchment (except their white turbans) gave a tremendous volley and then—turned tail! The wild 'Hurra' appeared to terrify them, and we rushed at the guns on the left flank of my Regiment which we spiked (six being taken by my little fellows and seven by the rest of the Brigade) and we kept continually pitching into the mass of broken Infantry flying sulkily to the river. The Lancers and Cavalry charged—the Infantry pushed on, the guns galloped to the Front, and poured in grape and shrapnel. Guns were spiking in all directions as the enemy relinquished them in their flight, and with shout and halloo we drove them bang into the Sutlej, their Cavalry treading down their own infantry in the river in the wildest confusion! Our guns drew up on the river side and blazed away into their panic-struck masses on the opposite bank, the Sikhs hurried away in utter dismay until not one was visible across the Sutlej as far as the eye could reach over the plain.

"The victory was *most complete*. We took every gun they had—69—all brass of large calibre and most beautiful pieces—all their immense magazines of powder and ball—all their large commissariat stores—the whole of their camp and camp equipage as it stood. Hundreds of camels, horses, and gun bullocks. The whole material of their army (provided for a march to Delhi ! ! !) In fact they took nothing with them except the wet clothes on their backs well ducked in the Sutlej.

"The whole thing was right well managed and though of course we have suffered still our loss is small compared to the brilliant result. It is I believe about 200 killed and 500 wounded, only five officers killed.

"Smallpage, of Hill's Irregulars, Capt. Grimes, 50th Foot, Lt. Swetenham and Cornet Williams of 16th Lancers, and Lt. Farquhar, 1st Cavalry. The Lancers suffered terribly: two officers and 65 men killed, six officers and 76 men wounded.

"My little fellows behaved beautifully; we were first into the entrenchment and spiked the first gun. We have been so much praised and buttered from the General commanding down to the private soldier that we hardly know whether we stand on our heads or our heels! The Lancers passed us on the field after the battle—drew up and gave the Gurkhas three hearty cheers—the 50th and the 53rd did the same at different times. I had some wonderful escapes and am grateful to a gracious God for preserving me. I had a grape shot through my coat, and a musket ball ditto, and a ball through my holsters, and the round shot knocked over men within a foot of me. Liptrot, my second in command, had his horse shot under him by a cannon ball, and the heel of his boot carried off by another. Reid, my Adjutant, had his horse hit by a round shot in his nose carrying away the check of his bit —but in person we are all untouched. The loss of *our* Brigade is *double* that of the whole of the Infantry *combined*. We have got in all the guns which were to be sent to Loodhiana and we shall then I believe move to Ferozepore. The Sikhs will never meet us on an open field again, depend upon it. We have captured a Col. Brown of the Sikh Artillery who deserted from our Artillery 15 years ago. He says the Sikhs were quite confident of licking us, and made no arrangements for retreat, but that the determined and steady advance of our Infantry against their tremendous Artillery so completely confounded and dismayed them that they became panic-struck. He says since the battles of Moodkee* and Ferozeshah there is a saying in the Punjaub that if 15 Sikhs were tied to a Sipoo tree and one European were to advance against them their struggles to get away from the Feringhee would pull the tree down: I fancy Col. Brown will be hanged as he was taken fighting against us. My little fellows have had hard work since the battle. We picked up all the guns from the river on the evening of the 28th, and have been daily at work ever since. We are now guarding the Fords with a Squadron of the 1st Cavalry (commanded by George Sandhorn), but Sir Harry told us yesterday: *I work you hard just now because I have dependence on you and you are the only light Bobs in camp, but you shall have plenty of holiday by and bye*. After that we cannot grumble. We all slept on the field of battle wrapped in our cloaks

* Now known as Mudki.

—and although hungry and cold we were as you may suppose as happy as Princes! Such a regular thrashing the Sikhs have not had as yet.

"Sam's wound has been very painful but is healing.

"Pray recollect that my letters are not for the papers. Sir Henry Hardinge is very particular on this point."

This letter is docketed: "Copy of letter from John Fisher, Commanding Sirmoor Batt. 2nd Gurkas, to Frederick Young, late 2nd Gurkhas, February, 1846."

In reading this account of the battle of Aliwal we enter into my Father's very heart *and the core of his life's deepest interests*. But John Fisher's optimistic faith was unfortunately not fulfilled. The scroll of Fate was still unrolled, and its unfolding held for him its special menace. The conflicting armies were to clash once more beside the Sutlej River.

The result of the complete defeat of Runjoor Singh at Aliwal by which the whole of the left bank of the Sutlej was entirely evacuated by the enemy was received with great joy by the Governor-General. His general order of that date expressed in measured terms his well-deserved praise extolling the conduct of all arms, and history adds these words "*The two Gurkha Regts. not yet enrolled among the Regulars of the Indian army had greatly distinguished themselves.*"

But the decisive struggle had yet to come. The reinforcements we had summoned all round were now arriving and concentrating; the Sikhs held a good position on the further bank, and were entrenching, on this side, the entrance to their bridge of boats, and their strongest point in command of the only available ford. In fact on both sides the conflicting bodies were as busy as bees in preparation.

General Wheeler had been left in command of a detachment guarding the fords by Aliwal, so that he was not taking an active part here; but the regiment which absorbs *our* interest was on this occasion brigaded with the 16th N.I. and that glorious regiment of unsurpassed records then known as 1st Bengal Fusiliers (now I think "The Munsters"), under the command of Brigadier Raleigh Gilbert, and was again occupying the centre in the attacking column. The full account of this battle is vividly interesting but I now confine my narrative to the point where our interest culminates. I cannot, however, refrain from quoting a passage in Sir C. Gough's book taken from the records of that great regiment I have mentioned, whose heroes of a later period were so well-known to me personally. It is a picture of the dawn of the 10th February, 1846.

> "The rising sun rapidly dispelled the morning mists and then a magnificent picture presented itself. Our batteries of Artillery were well in position ready to open fire: the plain covered with our troops the fortified village of Rhoda Walla on our left rear, being strongly held by our Infantry. Immediately our guns opened a heavy fire—the enemy seemed suddenly to realize their danger, their drums beat the alarm! Their bugles sounded to arms! And in a few minutes their batteries were manned and pouring shot and shell upon our troops. The scene suddenly transformed from the picturesque to the veritable earnest of war!"

In the course of the action the Commander-in-Chief, who fully realized the superiority of the Sikh weapons of artillery, may have given voice to his anxiety. But, however it may have happened, a rumour ran along the line that "old Gough," having been told that there only remained four rounds of ammunition per gun, said: "*Thank God I'll soon be at them with the bayonet.*"

Whether he actually said these words or not is, as his son says, "immaterial." The rumour filled the men with delight, and determination that such a move should not fail! Meanwhile Gilbert's division "*in the centre*" had encountered tremendous obstacles in the strong, high earthworks that had been skilfully built to guard the entrenchments. No scaling-ladders were at hand: twice they had to fall back but, persevering and mounting on each others backs, succeeded in gaining a footing in the entrenchments, the Sirmur Batt. leading and capturing the guns. This gallant charge is the culminating point in our interest and was, indeed, the beginning of the end of the great battle of Sobraon in which the whole Sikh army was utterly and irretrievably defeated. Alas! John Fisher could *not* write home the story of this day for, in their desperate final charge, leading and encouraging his men, he received the bullet in his head that instantly killed him; but it was remarked as extraordinary that, for an appreciable interval before he fell, he sat upright on his horse as if still leading, though his brave spirit had joined the other brave spirits on the further side. Not more than a fortnight had passed since he had written the story of the other battle, and thanked God that his life was spared. I do not suppose that letter reached my Father until after they knew that the hand that wrote it was stilled for ever.

The death of John Fisher was a greater sorrow than any that had gone before.

So ended the first Sikh war and my memories of how the news came home!

All that spring was spent in preparation for my Father's return to India, and it was decided that my three sisters should go out with him. My brother was placed at school in England, and my Mother and her three remaining girls were to occupy the house in Coleraine where my Aunt Barbara formerly lived.

So the scene changed once more.

The front windows of Ballysally commanded a view of the road that led to Coleraine until it reached the cross-roads leading to Portrush and the Giants' Causeway and, turning to the right, was hidden by the trees round Milburn House. From those front windows I watched the coach with its four splendid horses, and heard the sound of the bugle as, shedding copious childish tears and thinking I understood what sorrow meant, I saw one half of the old home-life torn off and carried away, and in the big house only the remnant left!

But the remnant was rich in balm and I was very young.

CHAPTER XI

Farewell to Childhood and the Dear Country

> "Pictures that cannot be washed out
> By all the drenching rain of life's wild storm."—*L.H.J.*

This short chapter is an interlude before continuing the story of my principal character.

There is a saying "home is where the heart is," and I may call this a farewell to home! In my 87 years of life I have never been more than five years in one place, and then it was more of a camp than a home and only portions of my heart were with me. Every Anglo-Indian will understand this. After the break-up of the household at Ballysally the little family left behind in Ireland soon changed their quarters, and the household was reduced to its small requirements. There was no longer a nursery, but a schoolroom and a governess, to whose beautiful memory I here pay my tribute! We were in the house in Coleraine where my Aunt Barbara and Susan Gage had lived latterly, and nearly everything in the living-rooms downstairs remained as they had left it. But the upper floors had undergone drastic changes. The two large front-rooms are shrines in my memory, the one my Mother's bedroom, the other the schoolroom. There was a large garden attached, with plenty of fruit and flowers, rowan trees, and laburnums.

We arrived there late one evening, in what Americans call "the fall of the year," and the days had begun to shorten. All was in order, and the workers resting—tired after a strenuous day. My Mother was taking her ease in the great arm-chair in her bedroom, and I was told to keep the children quiet downstairs for a little while: the room was very cosy with a window at either end and it held plenty of novelty for young explorers. After a little while I found an interesting book, and, as the room had not been lived in lately, a wood-fire had been lit in the grate, and I crouched down on the hearth to catch faint flares of light. The two little ones, tired of exploring, had resorted to that amusement which is the usual resource of restless youth—Hatton and Marion were laughing merrily and jumping up and down on the sofa near the wall! Thinking it was a forbidden game, and that I was neglecting my duty I said severely:

"I wonder what Aunt Barbara would say if she could see you?"

The words had hardly been uttered when on the wall behind the sofa there was a loud knock that resounded through the silence of the quiet home! I do not think one of the three children in that room doubted for an instant that Aunt Barbara *had spoken!* I know I was very frightened; the two culprits with a bound were beside me on the hearth and clinging to me; and there we sat until someone came to take us up to bed. On the other side of the wall was the entrance-hall and *no one had been there*. The relationship between me and "the children" was rather extraordinary. When danger threatened in any shape I was their stand-by, though in reality I was the greatest coward of the three—I may say "of the four," for the most firm believer in my heroism was my Mother. I never boasted, but I *never confessed*, so the strange myth took root!

I have said my young governess was beautiful to

me. Her name was Mary Lindsay—out of school my companion, in lesson-hours a power. I loved her dearly. She was my governess for one year only, but the foundation-stone of everything I have ever tried to know in history, in literature, in French, was laid in that dear Irish schoolroom. Of course she was the goddess in that shrine, but she was not quite alone! There was another object of delighted admiration whose coming (twice a week, I think) was hailed with joy. His name I am not sure of, but *he* —with his nimble legs, his bald head, his fiddle—and the rythmic glories and gambols of Irish jigs and reels can never be forgotten! How the windows rattled and the house shook when we "tuk the flure." There's only one country in the world that can give such memories to a child and even that may require a past tense in these degenerate days!

One other personal story for this chapter. Why do I tell it? It is certainly an unforgotten picture and it illustrates a truth—that love, and trust, and confidence in a child braces it to meet lions in the path.

I had a godmother who disliked me (not perhaps so much as I disliked her). She always tried to shake my Mother's belief in my pluck. *She was quite right* but, sooner than let her prove it, I would have died a thousand deaths! We had a large garden with a reputed ghost who used to wheel a barrow along one path, and could be distinctly heard but not seen, even if he passed you. That path overshadowed by trees, always dark and gloomy in the leafy summer, and with branches that whistled eerily in the bare winter-time, went past the wall that divided the stable-yard from the garden; and half-way in the length of it was a door (always locked at night) that led into the yard. At the time we had no carriage and horses, but the coach-house was used as a sort of store for boxes and surplus belongings, and in the yard was a stack of turf. One dark and stormy evening I had been looking out into the garden and wondering about the wheel-barrow (but, though I wondered about it, it was not the kind of thing that frightened me), and then Ellen came and closed the shutters and brought the light, and was followed by my Mother and *the godmother*. They had evidently been arguing—my heart beat. I knew why, as with a laugh the woman said:

"I don't believe you, and *you* are afraid to ask her to do it!"

My Mother put her hand on my shoulder. I knew she was angry for I felt her tremble, but she spoke —the truth.

"Louisa" (*i.e.*, my godmother) "says you would be afraid to go into the back-yard and see if the coach-house door is locked—would you?"

I do not remember what I said. I knew my Mother hated asking me to do it, but I braced myself to meet the trouble for her sake. No doubt I was in somewhat of a turmoil and hardly knew what happened until I found myself with a big key and a lantern— for it was pitch dark in that garden-path! I gained the door in the wall under the ghostly, groaning, autumn trees and fitted the big key into the lock. It is strange how thoughts come to one suddenly in moments of emergency, but I remember that before I pressed back the door over the gravel to prevent it banging in the wind I held the lantern high as I turned it on the yard that it might look as if held by a tall person! As I did so I heard a scrambling noise, and saw by the flash of the lantern light a figure vanishing over the top of the carriage-gateway that led to the road. I passed the turf stack, I saw the turves lying about, I laid my hand on the cold padlock, it was firmly fastened: and then—then I turned to come back!

Let any other cowards realize (for only cowards can) what it means to turn your back on a dark that is alive with horrors. There are no words to describe the appalling network of creeps formed by the nerves over your whole body, and especially down your spine! I shut the garden-gate and locked it—and when I came in past the wondering servants who had not been allowed to follow me I said: "The door is locked, but a man has been stealing turf; it's all lying about, I saw him get over the gate." And then—*I saw the triumph I had worked to gain, and all the torments of that time were forgotten.*

My legal baptismal name is Louisa. I detest it, but my dear godfather's name was Louis, and I always liked to call myself "Louise," and Louise I have been to many who loved me!

There is another sketch that belongs to this year. As my own experience—and seen as I paint it—it must be looked at with my young eyes as it just flashed in and out of this small period of my life.

She was called Mary Dhoon and my Aunts and cousins called her Dhoonie; she was the motherless child who had been sent home from India in 1814. It was a great treat to us to go and see her. She was like a princess. From what I can recall she lived in apartments in a street of big houses; I remember one old, devoted servant. Everything about her rooms was of the daintiest and best. She was always dressed in rich fabrics and her long thin fingers were covered with rings. She always wore a great deal of jewellery, just like a princess in a story, and there seemed to be nothing she did not know, nothing she could not do. I had a great respect for learning in those days, and I felt when in her presence that she was quite different to ordinary people, but my admiration was silent and restrained. She drew, and painted, and beautiful needlework filled her frames. She played and sang without effort, and read and spoke French and Italian. Of course we knew that she was delicate and often ill, and though she moved in an upright, regal sort of way I could not but notice a hesitation in her walk that betrayed a lameness she tried to hide. One touch that brought her nearer to me was her openly-expressed love and admiration for my Mother. She had many friends and visitors and it seemed to me that every one conceded to her a peculiar and superior position. Certainly no one I knew lived in the same luxurious atmosphere, and whatever destiny had ruled out from her life everything possible had been done to compensate her. Her deep contralto voice was a great pleasure to me but—*such is life*—when the magic spell of her presence was removed my irreverent nature expanded! To the delight of my sisters when we were playing "ladies" in the garden I used to try and reproduce some of her songs, amidst great applause. Especially:

"Some love to roam o'er the dark sea foam
Where the shrill wind whistles free,
But a chosen band in a forest land,
And a life in the woods for me!
Ho ho! ho ho! Ho ho! ho ho!
A life in the woods for me.

The deer we mark in the forest dark
And the prowling wolf we track,
But for right good cheer in the forest here
Oh! why should a Hercules lack?
Ho ho! . . . ."

The "Ho ho!" chorus in the *finale* was much appreciated.

So I give her as she stands in my gallery of vignettes. How long she lived and where she died, I do not know. I have lately seen in an old letter-book that my Father corresponded with her regularly.

This summer of 1847 has two vivid colourings. One sunbright and beautiful, and one in deep shadow, as shadows lie on one's youthful path. The shadows were round us, and often followed us in our daily life and our walk with Miss Lindsay. We would come home sad and depressed and found our best comfort in entering Betty's kitchen, and helping to carry big bowls of "brochan" (always on the boil) to poor famished miserables at the back-door, or even on the steps of the hall-door. It was the memorable year of the famine, when the potato-crop had failed: and even here, in the far-away and prosperous North, thin, half-clad ghosts of men, women, and children from the outskirts of the more afflicted districts were toiling along the roads and appealing to their more fortunate fellow-creatures. Yet—it was Ireland—and of the many episodes I might remember, one especially remains with "its tear and its smile." We had carried a bowl of porridge to a thin skeleton of a woman on the front doorstep and, having been taught that it was not polite to watch them eating, had retired, closed the door, and waited, for they always knocked to return the dish and spoon. This time the faint rapping came at once, and, on answering the call, a face with the ghost of a smile was raised, and a weak voice said:

"Sure, ye've left out the salt."

The sunshiny days were spent in picnics at the famous places on that grand coast. Far abler pens than mine have spread the fame of these spots, and, being works of nature, time writes no fading lines on them, though man makes an effort to do so. In 1847 "The Giant's Causeway" was open and free to all the wondering world. Now I believe there are fences and entries and something to pay at the gate. Oh, shades of my compeers, think of that!

I wonder if ghosts rise up, as of yore, from the Spanish galleon under the waves and wander in their old haunts in the dead of night? I wonder if some sombrero'd don has a wink in his eye as he approaches the hidden cave where, when I was young, those who liked could "taste a drop o' the craythur" without let or hindrance—no tales told. For I must believe that corner of mirth is still there, and I am sufficiently lawless to say "long life to it!"

Then there was a long and beautiful beach of "the White Rocks" with the snowy pebbles and the green fern-like seaweeds that cling to them. Looking down their length and crowning their final cliff was "Dunluce Castle." How thrilling the legends of its final fall and ruin! One picnic there is a picture in my collection—no fairy-scene, but a memory of those last home-days. I do not often recall such details, but I distinctly remember the bonnet my Mother wore that day. It was a mauve-grey straw with pale pink ribbons! I do not remember if many people were there. She sat on the green slope in the shadow of the broken walls, clasping the hand of one child beside her, whose most lovely face was looking up in rapt delight while she sang a song. I do not remem- that song—probably an Irish melody, for she knew them all—and I have heard from others that those words and that music in the open air was the melody my Father loved, and that the sound of it had often echoed in lovely, starlit nights among the distant

Himalayas! It echoes in my heart now as I bid farewell to the dear home and the beautiful land where nature has been so kind and so bountiful.

I must, however, include in my farewell a little sketch of a waif and stray who did not soon forget us. For many years afterwards my Mother used to get letters from him to which she always replied over the intervening spaces of land and sea.

His name was Archie O'Callaghan; he was a ragged waif and stray. Picture him standing on the pavement in front of the Inn in Coleraine Square—a thing of rags and tatters: before him in the road, the magnificent horses and faultless splendour of Sir Harvey Bruce's drag. Sir Harvey himself, fair-haired, rosy-faced, meticulously got-up in every particular, coming down the steps of the Inn, smilingly putting in the last button of his gloves. The urchin moves slightly—as if to let him pass with permission—and then, the ribbons correctly gathered, the whip in proper position, an almost stentorian voice says: "All right, Sir Harvey," and with a military salute Archie O'Callaghan dismisses the equipage! "All right, Sir Harvey" was a household-word in many Coleraine families. It remained in ours for many and many a day.

In the late autumn of that year a coach-and-four with sounding bugle-horn bore a miserable little girl, alone with strangers, on the road to Belfast, and the dividing seas. The world was changed.

CHAPTER XII

A Memorable Fact that should be Better Known: 1850

> "For most men, till by losing rendered sager,
> Will back their own opinion with a wager."

> "To hold converse with nature's charms
> And see her stores unrolled."

I come again to a misty period so far as my Father's personal narrative goes; but there is a light on the main points which shows his connection with the chapter of history on which I am going to touch.

When my Father, approaching his 60th birthday, landed in Calcutta in 1846, he was offered the command of the Ferozepore Brigade.

This was a compliment and a proof of the confidence and appreciation which was attached to his record of service. He accepted the offer at once, and, as it took him into the region of activities and responsibility in no small degree, no doubt it pleased him greatly.

I cannot describe the position better than by quoting the following extract written by one who knew and loved him :—

"This was a most important post, for there were murmurs of a second Sikh War, and as Ferozepore was our Northern Frontier in that country, he had not only to keep all troops ready for instant action, but to guard carefully against surprises and conspiracies."

My Father commanded this Brigade until the end of 1849. What is often spoken of as the Second Sikh War is, more properly, the Punjab Campaign. It included a large area, and, like a coming thunderstorm, its distant murmurs grew into reality at many remote points, before again concentrating in the familiar region of the five rivers. In the first war we followed its fortunes on the banks of the Sutlej, and now we are to trace the battles further north, on both banks of the Chenab past the Ravee —on which is Lahore—and approaching the Jhelum where it bends to the north.

With the more southern battles we have nothing to do, beyond the fact that they absorbed many needed troops and particularly that branch of arms without which our great chief, Sir Hugh Gough, Commander-in-Chief, felt that efforts were futile. We were fighting a brave enemy well-provided for the encounter, and superior to us, not only in the number of his guns, but in their calibre, and quality. Urged by the Government, blamed by would-be warriors from their easy-chairs in distant safety, Sir Hugh Gough and his gallant troops faced fearful odds. In reading history we gather the truth that the Israelites were by no means the only people who were expected to make "bricks without straw"!

Through both the wars in this region, the Commander-in-Chief had been demanding artillery to cope with that opposed to him, but, as a matter of fact, he had been obliged to do without it. His first battles in this second campaign presented very painful episodes, in most cases attributable to this want: that those episodes were not more severe (and they were even charged with the risk of finality

—not in our favour) was owing exclusively to the dash and courage of our men and their devotion to, and trust in, their noble commander, who many times placed his reputation in their hands. He was called reckless for so doing by those who could not grasp the fact that mutual sympathy and comradeship have irresistible powers. Only soldiers—those who serve and those who are served—understand the strength of that bond.

After the battle of Chillianwalla the Chief paused. Troops in the south were set free by the fall of Multan and he determined to take no more risks until reinforcements such as he had demanded were on the scene. Ignoring the hostile interpretations put upon his inaction, he persistently waited—but his waiting was not the inaction that his enemies represented it to be. Always in battle-array, moving from place to place as if undecided what to do, he utterly intrigued the foe as to his intended point of attack. Then, when the power he had demanded was in his control, there was no hesitation. He struck the final blow in confidence. Gujarat ended for all time that phase of strife.

On the 31st of March, 1850, Sir Hugh Gough wrote his farewell address to the army he loved.

The war was ended.

But the clash of arms had given way to the clash of opinions, as men of note came together to put their new house in order or, rather, to arrange order out of chaos through the labyrinth of conferences and the conflicting jars of civil and military contradictions. As the subject of discussion was how to decide the future of the Sikh's lost Kingdom I will quote here a tribute to the fallen foe, a fine tribute which was not only for that age but "for all time":

"In the hour of surrender, as in the hour of battle, they proved themselves a worthy foe—as, in the days to come, they were to prove themselves worthy comrades-in-arms."

There are many lesser celebrities who figure in history at this period, but to give the proper atmosphere of the times in relation to my own narrative I will take the liberty of indicating three principal characters who seem to represent broadly the currents of opinion swaying the conferences. I will label each of them with a short historical notice, and also quote their own words in support.

First of all there was Lord Dalhousie, Governor General: in his own words he was of the "strong and deliberate opinion that in the execution of a sound and wise policy the British Government is bound not to put aside or neglect such rightful opportunities of acquiring territory or revenue as present themselves."

Others held him to be "a man to whom it seemed obvious that extension of British rule was necessarily for the benefit of the ruled." Also:

"That the use of officers was to take their orders from him"; and that:

"The enemy deserved to be chastised for their insolence"!

Secondly there was Sir Charles Napier who had just been appointed Commander-in-Chief in place of Sir Hugh Gough. It was said of him: "There probably never existed a man more firmly convinced that he was right and every one who differed from him was wrong!" That he was a great soldier, deeds not words are his witnesses. But naturally he wanted to transform the Punjab into a military province. He was the Conqueror of Sind, and not long before had announced the fact in his memorable telegram *peccavi* (I have sinned). That civil rule should take precedence was a proposition that met with his utter disapproval.

The autocrats met—and at their first interview "told each other some home-truths." Sir Charles was an outspoken man, and he called Lord Dalhousie "the Laird o' Cockpen"; "a young Scotch Lord with no head for governing an Empire." What his adversary replied the record does not say; but the modifying influence in the situation was supplied by the

Third Man: the great and honoured Henry Lawrence. He was backed in his opinions by years of experience and successful work in the Punjab. No man knew better what he held broadly—that right action was:

"To deal generously with a noble though vanquished foe."

Henry Lawrence was a humble man who never advertized himself, but there is little doubt that his doctrine and above all his example and the wise acts and noble careers of the many disciples who followed in his footsteps, had a great deal to do with the successful result of a great undertaking, which in spite of conflicting ideas *was* an ultimate success. It seems presumptous on my part to pick holes in the garments of great men. But I do so because it throws the light I want on the true story of the next service my Father rendered to his country. It emphasizes the difference between civil and military method and the paradox that military experience leads to peace on some occasions, when civil autocracy would risk lives—for minor advantages. This incident is passed over in records and entered in Government schedules under a disguising heading. At the same time, if I seem to have spoken lightly of Lord Dalhousie, I must add here how warmly I appreciate his eminently distinguished administration, for in spite of our hot-headed but honoured Chief he proved that he certainly had the capacity for "governing an Empire." His parting words when retiring from the great work he had accomplished are worthy of the whole world's attention, and if universally acted upon, privately and politically, would do more than disarmament or any other scheme towards securing the world's peace.

"To fear God and have no other fear."

But to return to my story.

Naturally when a man has fixed opinions and finds himself opposed it rouses certain elements into activity, and the Governor-General was at that time very much irritated by the behaviour of another eastern potentate residing in a locality well-protected by natural barricades.

He refused to do what he was told! The well-known botanist Dr. (afterwards Sir Joseph) Hooker and a Mr. Campbell, a political resident, had penetrated into the fastnesses of the mighty Himalayas in the Kingdom of Sikkim while pursuing their harmless but most useful search among the flora of that region. They were at first most kindly received and so lured on into remote places. The story of their adventures is very interestingly given in *Life and Letters of Sir Joseph Hooker* by Mr. Leonard Huxley which has been published recently. The travellers came, however, to an uncomfortable point where they were made prisoners and forcibly detained, badly fed, and roughly treated. It had occurred to the Rajah, with the usual working of the eastern mind, that it was a good opportunity for demanding certain concessions, while he held the two Englishmen as hostages. Quite properly and naturally his proposals were ignored and the release of the prisoners peremptorily ordered. This order not being at once obeyed, and the Rajah continuing to try negotiations, the Governor-General ordered an expedition of British troops to be organized (for which seemingly *he* arranged the details). My Father on account of his former experience in hill-warfare was appointed to the command. In December, 1849, when proceeding with his staff to take up a brigade-command at Dinapore to which he had been appointed, his journey was diverted, and he was ordered to proceed at once to Darjeeling, and take up a new appointment as commander of the large force assembling there preparatory to an invasion of Sikkim.

The Rajah was still pugnacious and demanding his own terms: the Governor-General was also pugnacious, and determined not only to refuse demands but to administer punishment! The order was given for this large British force to advance into the Rajah's territory. Meanwhile the Rajah, alarmed by rumours of preparations, had released his prisoners and had sent them into Darjeeling.

In his journal of this date Dr. Hooker speaks of meeting my Father on his arrival, and begins by mentioning him in rather a slighting manner as "the old gentleman General Young" saying he seemed "in the clouds" and "all abroad" as to what he had to do. As I have said, my Father was a silent man on occasions. Dr. Hooker must have been a comparatively young man, and on the remote line of life, with all its absorbing interests, that he had followed, was perhaps not well-acquainted with military history of Northern India. He could not at once enter into the situation nor realize how well the "old gentleman" saw through the "clouds," nor how—in modern parlance—instead of being "all abroad" he was *very much all there!*—deliberating how to act in the most diplomatic manner while hesitating to comply with the imperious order he had received from the Government. Personally I have no doubt that at Headquarters he had many friends who would testify to his knowledge, experience, and wisdom. The Rajah had no army, but he had rocky fastnesses, many natural barriers, and a most inclement climate, arctic in its severity. Of course a soldier's duty is to obey, but, in a momentous crisis like this, when the lives of hundreds of gallant men were seemingly about to be rushed into certain danger, prompt obedience was a debatable question. Of course he was risking much, under the circumstances, in proposing a milder course before resorting to extreme measures, but he was in a position from his personal knowledge to point out the difficulties that faced such an expedition, at that season especially. His evident idea was to commence the advance (*which he did at once*); to terrorize the people, and through them the Rajah, by display of strength; but at the same time to demand certain concessions *from* the Rajah as punitive measures instead of conceding to his demands; and on condition of his acceptance of these terms to stay the invasion of his country. And in considering these facts we must not forget that just as his experience in hill-warfare had been recalled by those who selected him for this command, so also his own repute among these hill-tribes, and the confidence and affection he had secured from some among them, were important factors in the negotiations. For his own satisfaction he wrote a report to his own chief—the Commander-in-Chief of the army—asking his opinion. There is no copy of the letter my Father wrote, but this was the reply :—

"Headquarters Camp,
"20 February, 1850.

"I have read your letter through the Adjt.-General of the Army. I entirely approve of your plan of advance as stated in your letter 31 January, from Darjeeling.

"I consider that the enterprise entrusted to you by the Government is a very hazardous one and judging from Mr. Lushington's letter, I should say that it was impracticable.

"I am too ignorant of the country to presume to offer you any advice. Your own judgment seems excellent, and I should say has prevented a great disaster.

"I imagine you will be ordered to advance; I do not think the Governor General will allow his threats to the Rajah of Sikim to fall as harmless words but in that case, your force must be increased.

"Yours faithfully,
"C. J. Napier, Commander-in-Chief."

This letter must have heartened him. After all, he was a military man—under civil orders!

Dr. Hooker continues in his journal of a later date :

"I went down with the troops the other day —they took possession of the Bridge over the Great Rungeet, and camped some 500 men in Sikim—no further advance at once—but—the orders are to *march* to Tumlong and occupy the capital."

From this it is plain that the public were not in my Father's confidence! The result shows that this bit of bluff succeeded.

The only remark relating to the transaction in a private letter is:

> "The Rajah has given in. He gave your Father a great big elephant that carried some of his camp equipage through the Terai. It was in the compound afterwards at Dinapore, and was amusing to watch."

But in a foot-note to Dr. Hooker's journal is a paragraph from some current newspaper which says:

> "The expedition was abandoned because the General from his experience in the Nepaul campaign reported the country as impracticable for British Troops."

Also Dr. Hooker in a letter to his mother says:

> "That a very carefully prepared map of his travels intended for her, was given by him to General Young."

I much regret that this valuable document has vanished with all the other lost papers that belonged to my Father.

I have spoken of the entry in a Government schedule in reference to this episode.

In one vol. of a series entitled *Rulers of India*, and written by Sir W. Hunter is this grandiloquent phrase, in speaking of the detention of Dr. Campbell and Sir Joseph Hooker:

"A military expedition thus became necessary, and a submontane strip of inconsiderable extent together with certain hills was exacted from the Rajah by way of punishment and fine."

Nothing is said of a great disaster averted!

Once more I am so thankful that my memory can give a picture of that "*submontane strip of inconsiderable extent.*" Although in drawing that picture I am weighed down with regret that, when I looked upon it one memorable day in 1870, while stationed at Darjeeling, I did not know that my Father had been there. Not one of the party who picniced on the banks of the Great Rungeet on that occasion—military man or civilian—even recalled the fact that twenty years before 500 British troops had crossed that bridge and been encamped on the further shore to strike fear and awaken wisdom in the heart of a Sikkim Rajah. However, that visit comes back to me now so that the past becomes the present, and I can clearly perceive the "great disaster" that one man's courage and initiative turned aside from hundreds of brave men who hardly realized the escape they had, any more than Dr. Hooker realized what the "old gentleman in the clouds" was devising to safeguard his fellow-men. But it was done.

This, then, was the great bridge—the gateway into Sikkim from our side. And it was pre-eminently *the* bridge, a monster-work compared with others in the interior. Other great rivers have been crossed by clever engineering in many makeshift ways, but this—one of the greatest of rivers—was not a wide, deep-flowing stream with cross-current and eddies to be fought. It was a mountain-torrent all the way across from one bank to the other, and never knew a moment's peace—dashing and foaming in and out of huge boulders of rough rocks! Regularly every year this bridge had to be rebuilt after the rains, when the floods and melted snows had done playing with it. And the bridge itself—what was it? I will try to describe it.

Two sturdy, deeply dug-in and secured poles, rising considerably above the level of the torrent, stand on either side of the main banks, and bound to them are very strong, hand-made ropes that reach across the water. On these horizontal ropes loops of rope are fastened at intervals of two to three feet, and a strong plank of wood is interlaced in the lowest curve, as far as its length will go, fastened down and kept in place by basket-work of bark and grasses on either side to about a foot in height; so a man standing on the plank is in a kind of long-shaped cup and has the main ropes just about the height of his elbow. I know so much about it because I watched the men working; they had prepared it half-way across to the centre of the torrent with one or two lengths of fixed plank and a commencement of basket-work on one side. This platform for their further work was quite firm.

It was a wonderful expedition from Darjeeling; the road by which we came became such a steep descent that sitting on the saddle I had to bend back so uncomfortably that I very soon preferred my own legs. Besides that, it gave me a better opportunity to attend to the marvellous beauties of the road-side. We were passing through a thick forest of trees, and all about were ferns, and flowers, and grasses, and butterflies of every size, and all the treasures of a seldom-trodden pathway through the rare attractions of a wild Himalayan rock-garden. As the trees became less crowded we caught glimpses of the mighty mountains in Sikkim territory; but the grandeur and the colouring of such scenes have been described by so many worthy pens that I leave them to the imagination here. When the road ended we emerged on a beach unlike any beach I have ever seen. I do not know if it has been described before, but I imagine it was part of that "*sub-montane strip.*" It is a wide beach sloping upwards to the river-bank; at least it was so the year I saw it, but probably it alters every year when the flood comes, and probably forms part of the river-bed at high-water. The *pebbles*—water-polished bits of strange rocks, wonderful in variety and colour! My passion for stones and the secrets of geology had not then developed or my luggage would have been embarrassed with a sackful! Though at the time I never thought of all the things that hide in such fragments I look back with regret on the blind ignorance with which one walks through the great world. One thing however I do recall—it was so remarkable I could not but remember. Mingled with the unknown debris were pieces of malachite large and small.

On the landward edge of that beach we pitched our tents for the night. But the bridge had a powerfull attraction for me. We walked to the top of the bank where it started, and watched the grand swirl of waters rushing below and heard its loud song. I knew the bridge was quite safe; I had seen men and women squatting in the middle at the basket-work, and I had an irresistible impulse to walk to the end.

I did it: no one else followed my example: they called me foolhardy, but I am far too great a coward for that. I am never giddy, and I had ropes to hold to on either hand. In spite of its formidable unfinished appearance it was safer than many a simple plank I had crossed, and I am so glad to remember that high above the water I looked down on the centre of the Great Rungeet near its junction with the Teesta, and can now, in the light of past history, realize one at least of the insurmountable difficulties that prevented the road between Bhotan and Sikkim from being used as a road for a fully-equipped army with its cavalry and heavy guns!

That beach led away to the right in the direction of Tibet, and as far as we went we saw high ground rising between us and the river. Of course I do not *know*, but if this rising ground was part of the "outlying district" conceded to us it may have been for useful purposes.

This is my true and reliable story of "the military expedition which became necessary," and of the "submontane strip of inconsiderable extent together with certain hills exacted from the Rajah by way of punishment and fine."*

I think it is a story that should be better known as history.

* Sir William Hunter's book *Dalhousie* (*Rulers of India* series), p. 108. As in the case of "The Affair of Budhowal," there is no official record of this fact, nor is it mentioned in any private correspondence that I have been able to trace.

CHAPTER XIII

Seventy Years Ago

"Through all the changing scenes of Life."

When my Father left Darjeeling with his staff—his camp-equipage following, the tents carried on the Rajah's big elephant—his active soldiering was ended, and his remaining years of peaceful duties were spent by one who, though out of the hurly-burly, took a deep interest in public life at home and abroad and kept wonderfully in touch with the rapid march of things in general that took place in the latter half of the nineteenth century.

But the command of the large brigade in Dinapore and the district, though it was to him more in the nature of a show-parade, was also a very responsible post.

The picturesque part of it was described in a letter, written by my Mother, to the children in England who knew nothing about soldiers, while to her this phase of it was quite novel and unlike any of her former experiences in the beautiful northern valley where she had spent so many happy years. She, as I have said, was an exceptionally fine rider, and after describing her favourite mount, she says:

"Your papa looks very fine on parade. His charger is a handsome white Arab, and with the rich saddle cloth, and gold lace and all the corners embroidered in gold it is a very gay affair! I attend all the reviews and inspections of troops with him and his staff. It is most amusing to see his five Officers, all in cocked hats—dashing about after him! My horse always fidgets as if he thought he should be leading too! The last morning I was out all the Regiment drew up in line to salute, and the Bands struck up to play 'God Save the Queen' all together. I could not help laughing. The discord was great—one little fife playing louder than the others—and one big drum quite silent. Indeed it made all the officers smile; there is another monster review to-morrow and of course I am going to it."

Later on, I myself had the pride and privilege of seeing my Father "take the salute." Photography for amateurs was not yet, so I can leave no adequate replica of the picture that is unfaded in my mind, and no one is left alive now who could witness to its truth. The upright, soldierly figure; the graceful, white charger, thrilling with life and longing for action, but kept tremblingly still by the master-hand that held the reins; the noble face of the rider, with the fearless eyes and the uncovered glory of abundant silvery hair brushed straight up from the broad, full forehead. No wonder I was proud to know "that is my Father!"

The district in the Dinapore division was very extensive, including many principal towns with their garrisons, all demanding military supervision. This necessitated considerable time spent in inspections during the glorious climate which is winter-time in India. These tours under canvas were a pure delight to all who shared them! Of course the luxuries of a general's camp-equipment is to be considered, for it annihilated all the minor worries and inconveniences of smaller establishments. Everything was in duplicate so that tents struck on, say, Monday, when vacated were carried on for two marches and were ready-pitched and in order when the family arrived on Wednesday morning: and on arriving it seemed as if some fairy-carpet had transferred your canvas home *just as you left it* into its new surroundings, for the camps were pitched absolutely by measurement on the same plan. Every sleeping-tent had its bathing-enclosure enclosed by high walls (or *kanaughts*), but all uncovered to the clear sky. What could excel the joys of a big bath on a sunny morning after the ride of a long march (for with rare exceptions the saddle was the mode of transit)? And what could be more favourable to the enjoyment of a plenteous breakfast, with fresh fruits and every other appetizing accompaniment?

The dining-tent like all the others had double *kanaughts*, leaving a roomy verandah all round. The doorways were provided with reed-curtains called *chicks*, which admitted air and light but kept out flies and other winged depredators. Then the wonderful domestic household of those days! How they came and went, one never knew. They were always there, an innumerable army of them, but each one in his place, never tumbling over one another, or relegating their duties to anyone else.

The kitchen-tents were in duplicate like all the rest. The headman or *khansama* had his own army of officers, rank and file; he was responsible for them and all their works. He himself always kept in touch with the Sahib and his family, either preceding or following them *en route*—but *without visibility!* One of the wizard-touches in this business was that the personal attendants in the catering-department were always clothed in spotless white!

The kitchen might be located at some distance from the dining-room, but under all circumstances—even the rare, but occasional, downpour of a winter rain storm—the paraphernalia of the well-furnished table would be always up to *time*, and up to temperature; there were no cold dishes that should be hot, and, there was nothing in the calm, clean attendant to remind you that he had been working under unusual conditions. This marvellous white magic in an Indian camp is just as great a problem as any more pretentious feat of jugglery. Of course the orderly-room had its own perfect merits: but the crowning beauty of the moving palace was the drawing-room for the ladies and for the reception of visitors, who were numerous in certain localities. It was a large, square room called a *shamiana*. It had a canvas roof with wonderful colouring and a deep, gay fringe-border all round; it was open to the air on all sides but so-placed as to get the pleasant shade of trees at midday. There were softly-cushioned couches and easy-chairs and writing-tables and every civilized adornment. Always flowers—and thereby hangs a tale of Indian life! Everyone has a gardener. It does not matter if there is a garden or not. It is his duty to provide flowers even in an arid waste. You never ask where he gets them—that would not be playing the game!

This is a brief note as to what camp-life means to scores of civil and military men in India—but perhaps I should say *meant*, for I expect that in this perfect phase it is becoming a thing of the past. Those who knew it before modern innovation tasted a full cup of joyous life: I am sorry for the younger generation.

In 1852 my Mother died.

MRS. YOUNG, at the time of her marriage, 1825.

From a painting on ivory.

[*face p.* 160

One or two of my sisters were generally with my Father to help him with those social duties which are incumbent on a man in his position whatever his own inclination may be.

In the late autumn of that year I went out to India in the charge of my uncle, Colonel Louis Bird. An account of that journey may have interest because it contains some of those vanished scenes that are almost forgotten.

Of course the first sight of Gibraltar and Malta will always be "first sights" to young, untravelled eyes, and to depict the chief difference between the harbours of *now* and *then* would require more knowledge and skill than I can bring to bear on the subject. No doubt the sea-going craft in the old harbours were more picturesque than the monsters that have taken their places, and Valetta was less crowded than now, and one had time to realize its grand beauty. The one incident at Malta that I remember in 1852 I never tried to renew in all my subsequent visits, and whether the grim picture survives as yet, I do not know. It was an underground room in the old and beautiful church at Valetta, where a very weird assembly received us. They were *dried monks*, each standing in his own niche in the surrounding wall, dressed in the garb he wore in life. I never liked to look at disagreeable things, and I have kept no memory of details, except that our guide took some astonishing pride and comfort in the idea that some day he would join the assembly. He was a very shrivelled-up man and his aspiration seemed likely to be fulfilled! It was wonderful, no doubt, but I enjoyed much more the beauty of the historical building that stood above them.

Now, when you reach the African coast, you are

borne on the top of modern transit-machinery to continue your inland journey, and except for what you see through windows you might almost forget you were in a strange land. In those days it was different. When we arrived at Alexandria the stormy seas intervened between us and the harbour—and what a tossing we had while waiting. I know we saw the ship's boat (I think she was going for a pilot) capsized, and all the crew struggling in the water; but eventually something conveyed us to the landing-place, and to the places of new embarkation.

In those days there was no canal—no railway. We found ourselves on small boats that had to carry us to Cairo. How I wish I could accurately recall the business-details of this journey, but I know that we travelled in what everyone called "Nile boats," and that we landed every now and then to have food (a sort of scramble for what we could get, leaving the impression that nature was sustained on dates and nuts), and that we liked it, and laughed, and were merry. I cannot tell what was the motive-power that carried us on—sails, or oars, or towing ropes? I only know that to me, and I fancy to most of my young companions, it was one succession of varied delights. The immense dome of sky, unlike any other skies; the changing colours everywhere; the queer faces of the people; the beautiful blue of their *galabeyahs*; the fruits, the nuts, the glorious air, and clear atmosphere! And it was the Nile—the Nile that Cleopatra had known! Apart from those reminiscences it had its own peculiar charms—pictures on its banks that came and went far too quickly and made me long to linger at each bend. There were graceful women carrying brass, or red-earthenware, water-vessels on their heads, and bronze children clinging to their skirts, mostly naked or adorned with some patch of rag or bright colouring. I remember the *devices for drawing water*—the long, mysterious arm that bent over the river and as if by magic raised the full and overflowing buckets of water that gurgled into some receptacle with the rhythmic creak and chant of unseen pulleys. Then, near the scattered villages, were bright green patches of new vegetation, and groups collected on the banks to stare at our passing fleet; there were shepherds with their little flocks, and the bleating of animals that mingled with human voices.

This is what I recall of my first journey from Alexandria to Cairo. Of course at Cairo there was Shepheards Hotel. Yes, even then, 70 years ago! But I cannot trust my first memory of Shepheards; it would be all mixed up, for I have seen it so many times since then. But the first sight of the bazaar and the market still stands out as something unique that can never be renewed; certainly it is far enough away in the past to banish the thought of flies! I look past that plague, and see Cairo in all its beauty and novelty as if I had walked into the magic land of some eastern story. The wonderful work and draperies that overflowed every stall; the bright gleams of brass and steel and copper; the solemn, cross-legged men that sat amongst their brilliant goods, like Buddhas in a shrine, calmly listening to the excited admiration of their visitors; the strong, pervading smell of sandal wood and attar (*without the associations of the long years in eastern lands*). In all it is a gorgeous scene that no words can describe adequately. By degrees I have seen this old picture pass off the screen. Aniline dyes and cheap shams have flooded the old true market, and as a genuine article only the *Mussarabeeyah* work remains and very little of that. Glorious specimens have been torn away from their original surroundings leaving boarded gaps in the old proud houses in the disfigured streets. Some is still in the country, as at Mena House Hotel near the Pyramids, but Cairo itself has been robbed and defaced. That time we did not see the Pyramids nor the Sphinx, but we had the good fortune to do what no traveller of the P. and O. Company can do now—we travelled from Cairo to Suez across the desert in a camel-caravan!

The cars we travelled in were like small omnibuses with seats for six persons, and ours held my uncle and aunt, two girls (also under their care), myself, and a Mr. Le Bas, of the Indian Civil Service. My uncle had left the arrangements to him, and he, being an old traveller though an active and energetic young man, had engineered the whole thing beautifully. I expect that a considerable *douceur* went to the driver, but the result was that our van *held the rear*, so that the camels and their odour and the gurgling of their voices went before instead of following after. We started after dark, and never shall I forget that night of stars! Mr. Le Bas and I had the two end seats by the door (which was never closed), and he sat mostly on the step. He entered heartily into my enjoyment and was a delightful companion, for he knew when to refrain from speech and not break the great and beautiful silence when we lingered in the rear—for wheels in *the sand make no noise*. Our four companions slept most of the time. And then, the dawn! That rainbow-dawn over the desert-horizon—the few moments of incomparable beauty that come, and are gone! As day broke, little patches of vivid green proclaimed a growing world, and very soon the halt had dropped a curtain over what was passed.

The next scene in the drama was the halt—the

dust; the noise of men and camels; and the ejaculations of the re-united travellers, mostly exchanging sympathies over hard seats and jolting vehicles and all the horrid trials of a "night in a caravan."

Probably a great many had felt as I did, but I was very fortunate in having had a congenial companion who was conscious of the beauty of it all, and enabled me to guard, until this day, the memory of that *dream-night in a camel-caravan.*

This halt was Suez. Then came the long sea-picnic down the Red Sea and in the calm, untroubled Indian Ocean, enjoyed with all the light-hearted merriment of girls and boys just entering life and looking into the future as into a garden of roses—all waiting for them to pick and choose!

My Father met me in Calcutta; on his lavish goodness and generosity I need not linger. All who have followed my story so far will easily understand: it could not have been otherwise. To give freely and contribute to the happiness of others was an inalienable part of his nature.

I think it is well worth while to record how the journey progressed from Calcutta to Dinapore. It is a long time since the manner of it became a record of the past. The distance was considerable. It was not a good season for the river-journey, for my Father was anxious to return to his post and sandbanks and shallows caused delay even after the advent of the river-steamer; so there remained the journey by road. The road was the Grand Trunk Road; it had taken many years and very clever engineering skill to develop it, and it was almost perfect. But still some difficult places remained, such as the crossing of rivers and unstable links in its continuity that required mending after heavy

M

rain. At some seasons it was feasible to employ horse-carriages but otherwise travellers had to be contented with *coolie* substitutes. This year the rains had been heavy and my Father's experience had convinced him that, alhough he, travelling light, had taken horse-*dak* over the route, it would be undesirable with heavy luggage and women-passengers. So it was settled that as we could not use horses we should employ *coolies*. The two girls who had been my companions on the voyage were also going up-country to their parents, and my Father had offered to escort them the greater part of the way.

It will require a little exercise of the imagination to realize the component parts of our strange procession—for such it really was. Anything more novel and merry and luxurious it would be hard to describe. Having experienced the difference between then and now, between the barbaric and the civilized, I should still choose to be a barbarian! (In spite of the fact that no magnate in an eastern government has experienced the full advantages of modern resources more fully than I have in later years).

The carriages in which we then travelled were really like very roomy four-wheelers, the ordinary *dak gharri* of to-day being a very bad caricature of its predecessor. The doors were sliding panels, the upper half being *jhilmils* or venetian blinds. All round were cunning shelves and trays, and there was a large recess under the coach-box (the whole softly cushioned and pillowed) big enough to contain a small box holding your own resources. The centre-board was movable if you wanted to sit up; the luggage was so arranged on the top as to make a pleasant nest for the *ayah* and her bundles. In my case a trustworthy *chaprasseee* or *peon* occupied the coach-box; the twenty-five men who composed my team in relays did not require any one handling reins or whip! But this individual in snowy garb with brilliant official badge was a potentate with acknowledged power.

My carriage led the way; the two girls in one carriage followed; and my Father brought up the rear —three carriages each with its long, human team.

At certain distances we, so to speak, changed horses. To jaded travellers on the road, the noise, the dust, the strident voices talking in a strange tongue, might have been termed disturbing incidents, but to us it was all life and stir so different to any previous experience that the novelty made it a perpetual amusement. The brown, shiny, half-naked men (their *colour supplied clothing*) squatting down directly they were off duty and drinking from the quaint, metal cups they carried in some mysterious way roped round their waists; the quaint water-carrier who hastened to fill their cups; the eager mouthfuls of refreshment they extracted from tied-up corners of their scanty raiment and tossed into their mouths from the palm of the hand; the vendors of different eatables that collected round the group; the quarrelling; the counting out of *pice*, that queer money we saw for the first time! Then the men in authority who swaggered about and helped to harness fresh two-legged animals to their appointed places! These important persons were generally clothed in something that was, or had been, of brilliant colour and gave variety to the broad tint of brown that prevailed. And we were young, and the sun shone brightly, and generally great trees showed up against a clear sky, for nearly all the villages were amidst the trees. Women, too, would come, adding to the chattering and screaming voices, mostly with naked, wise-looking babies sitting astride on their hips, or native children in native bronze clinging to their skirts. The women were always fully dressed, their graceful *chudders* giving lines of beauty to the moving scenes.

There were no Savoy or Ritz palaces on the Trunk Road! But no such palaces in any great city I have visited have ever conveyed to me the joy and delight—the true sense of rest—that I found in the *dak bungalows* on the Trunk Road in that far-away lap on life's fairy-journey. Our course was so arranged that breakfast and dinner were not interfered with. At nightfall we punctually arrived. Each carriage was furnished with a bugle-horn, and the merry "hoot-toot" proclaimed our approach and drew the domestic establishment to the verandah of the rest-house to receive us. Foremost among them was the *khansama*; very often at that time he was an old and aristocratic chief who had moved in the best society, and received this coveted post in reward. It was just a square bungalow with wide verandahs and two or three suites of rooms. It was here I first realized the magic of the east. We, personally, said nothing, did nothing, asked no questions, gave no orders. We just stepped out of our carriages and before we had done more than greet each other the *ayah* had made a bare room into a comfortable dressing-room, and hot baths and clean towels and clean clothes were ready for us to dress for dinner. And such dinner! And such appetites! And my Father was as young as we were, and interested in all our chatter and amused with our amusement. When it was time to resume our journey (and his old bearer was a living clock) we went into our rooms, slipped into night-gowns and dressing wraps, and lo! the carriages that had been like a living-room all day with books, or work, or writing materials all at hand, had been transformed into luxurious beds where we could sleep the sleep of health and youth when the excitement of the changing scene allowed it. For now in lieu of sunshine there were torches that lent a new, weird beauty to the scene, flashing with a blinding brilliance or veiling in smoke the motley groups. The doors of course were closed, but the venetian blinds could be opened or shut at will. However, as we moved on our way sights and sounds soon merged into the silence and quiet, until another day and another transformation-scene were enacted! After breakfast (such breakfasts as I have never known since) we came back into our drawing-rooms and continued the journey.

The wife of the millionaire travels in her well-furnished car with maid and footman following, but could I put myself in her place I should never find again the joys of my barbaric tour outside civilization in that brief burst of golden spring.

I do not remember how long the journey took.

CHAPTER XIV

Some Phases of a Fine Character

> " He was a man, take him for all in all,
> I shall not look upon his like again."

If the time between my arrival at Dinapore and my Father's departure for England were not chronicled in known dates it would seem to me a *decade* at least: but it was only a short period of about fifteen months. Therefore, if this chapter in my memoir is very short, its value must not be measured by its brevity; the reader must remember the difficulty of condensing in this little space of time a fitting record of the varied revelations of a gifted and most lovable personalty.

My veneration for my Father had been with me always, and it never occurred to me that he could be otherwise than superior to other people, looking at the question in a general way. But it was now that generalities merged into particulars. Soldiering in peace-time may be dull but it gives moments of leisure. These made it clear that *that* was only one phase of my Father's character; apart from the soldier, the other half had an opportunity of declaring itself. The noble figure on parade, the courteous host in full panoply on great occasions, was a never-to-be-forgotten view; but the other side was so various, so full of unexpected surprises, that it took at once the higher place. To begin with, he was a very clever draughtsman. When I arrived at Deegah,

I saw in front of each fire-place in that big house (there was a fireplace in every room though fires were *never* wanted) large square pictures to block out the ugly cavity. They were mostly copies of well-known drawings in black and white with the light and shade beautifully balanced and the true perspective maintained: this was my first intimation of his hidden talent in this art, which was one of my own budding ambitions. I remember also on an easel a large picture he was copying from a small engraving, and trying to reproduce in colour. It was Uncle Toby and the widow, from Tristram Shandy, and occasionally—brush in hand—he would severely criticize his performance, and apostrophize his two subjects, making witty and amusing remarks.

The Poet has said

> "Distance lends enchantment to the view."

This is palpably true in its material and artistic conclusions; but to the mental view distance in time has deeper and more wonderful colouring to give, and looking back now from this distance I do not speak as I would have spoken then; I was still in my teens, I had led a very narrow and fenced-in life, my growth was slow, and I did not meet intelligently the sudden change in the conditions of life.

After my marriage in June of that year we lived in the cantonments for a few weeks, and then returned to Deegah—as the General's house was called—my husband being appointed the General's A.D.C.

My husband was tall and broad, a fair, good-looking man, with very fine blue eyes, a typical Englishman, and a good cricketer. He was a great favourite, very popular in society, with charming and attractive manners, and eminently fitted for this post. He had also passed more examinations in native languages before he was twenty-three than any other man in the service except the chief examiner in Calcutta. This is a record; I do not think it has been beaten.

In spite of the strenuous work of his early years, my Father had educated himself and kept ahead of most of his contemporaries in knowledge of the moving scenes of the times, and he maintained a fair level in all branches of intellectual progress, His general information was astonishing. He never drew attention to himself or criticised others. In literature or history—ancient or modern—if a subject were broached he could generally answer a question; but he never contradicted or took part in arguments, and plainly showed his distaste for heated discussions. Gay and debonair in society, going through with it as if he stood on the same level, he was far removed from the ordinary standard of those around him. He was really only himself when all conventional trammels were cast aside and he could revert to congenial occupations. His days were always full.

In a detached bungalow near the house, was a spacious, well-appointed billiard-table, and in smaller rooms near it he kept what he called his messes. Here he followed various pursuits in handicrafts of all kinds: he carpentered and carved and rigged model boats. He never indulged in the universal practice of the afternoon *siesta*, even in the hottest weather, but indulged, rather, in exercise at his billiard-table, clad in the lightest garments; they were English garments always, for in those days the adoption of that eastern costume now so frequently worn—even by women—was considered effeminate and unworthy. Once a new arrival in the drowsy East, not having assimilated the customs of the country, rode from the cantonments in the blazing afternoon to report himself. Some sleepy or stupid *chaprasssee*, probably the only member of the establishment who was awake, took the visitor across to the billiard-room. When the A.D.C., disturbed in his sleep, hastily put on some clothes, and, no doubt using very strong language, rushed across to attend to his duties, he found the General with the local newspaper unfolded to its utmost extent and held before him like a workman's blouse or apron to disguise his gossamer attire, entertaining a stranger in his usual courteous manner! The shy youngster who had so unwittingly intruded at closed hours, stood speechless from confusion! I have no doubt he was quickly put at his ease.

That billiard-room was a very favourite resort of young and old in the garrison and in the large civil station of Patna not very far-off. To many people a game here was a serious matter, like playing a champion, for the General was hard to beat.

There was one amusement my Father loved and excelled in. It was the play of the magic lantern. He had a beautiful apparatus, the best obtainable in Calcutta, with innumerable slides of every description, and he gave wonderful entertainments. But the bought slides did not satisfy his artistic tastes and requirements, and he produced new ones of his own workmanship, painted with transparent colours on talc; they were very beautiful and effective on the screen, without the stiff lines and the crude and untrue colouring of the regulation slides, and introduced new and popular subjects. Alas! I do not know what became of them all, but I am happy to have *one*, saved by some miracle when I lost most of my possessions during the mutiny. It is one of Landseer's stags and, though a good deal crushed and broken and originally a rejected copy, it bears worthy witness to the excellence of the workmanship.

Boys and young men loved his society. They never tired of hearing his tales of sport and adventure in untravelled wilds with that family of little Highlanders who were always so dear to him, and whose memory through many trials was unstained to his latest days! His Irish love of mirth and laughter made him a most desirable companion. Yet, though he met them on their own ground and made them feel at home, he never lost the power—it might be by simply lifting up a hand, or by a change in his voice, or even by a brief silence—of fixing the limit beyond which mirth should not go.

And then he had his large sailing-boat on the Ganges. The great river flowed past the house—often very near to it in flood time—and it was his great delight to sail her himself and take his friends on river-parties, and always on those occasions he had some new and wonderful invention to add to their pleasure or comfort or surprise. The path from the house to the river-bank ended in steps that led down to the landing-place, and on great occasions these were covered with red cloth, and his crew in spotless uniforms with private badges on their head-gear made the scene very picturesque.

We must not forget his stable of fine horses and no one could show them off to better advantage than he. I never remember him driving his own carriage-and-four, but I have seen well-known hands upon the reins—notably those of the Nimrod of that time, Colonel Bill Apperley of the Stud at Poosa, who was famous in his younger days for having driven a spirited tandem, with only a whip and no reins, over a narrow bridge leading to Fort William in Calcutta.

This is my vignette of fifteen full months at Deegah,

Dinapore, 70 years ago. It was the longest period in my life in which I had a close personal consecutive enjoyment of my Father's society, the deprivation of their natural rights being one of the penalties that lie so heavy on Anglo-Indian children and their parents.

In the beginning of 1854 my Father retired, after fifty-four years of service, with only one break of two years' furlough taken when he was nearly 60 years of age. And again the home was broken in two, and wide seas rolled between the fragments.

CHAPTER XV

True History: 1857.

What am I? Nothing. . . .
But not so art thou soul of my thought
With which I traverse Earth.

The continuation of my story, regarded as a memoir, is very feeble and intermittent, and will truly take its place in a gallery of vignettes for it is a broken line of narrative, now here, now there, as the writer records scenes in past history that may have a certain interest. The chain of association with the chief character, however, is never broken. His figure dominates the whole as the beautiful, steadfast background of the beacon-light of "home" to an unresting wanderer.

My Father on retirement settled in Ireland but not near his old home. The old landmarks had been removed by death and time. It held for him only reminders of the past; so he took a farewell view of familiar places in their changed aspect, and decided to live among the beauties of his favoured country, but well-removed from the North, and its surroundings.

Being attracted by the spell of the Wicklow Mountains, he finally decided to settle in that neighbourhood. The home in which I next found him, after the lapse of three-and-a-half memorable years, was a fascinating little nook called Fairy Hill, near Bray; but before that happened, both for him and for me and for all our family, the scene in life's drama had suffered several sad changes.

The record again calls for history, and with much reluctance I take up the thread of the narrative,with this drawback, that it is only *my* experience that fills a good deal of the programme.

My dear Father in settling down to his changed life preferred the quiet of home to society. He was now 70 years of age and beginning to suffer from deafness, that terrible calamity of old age: it is looked on by the young as matter of course, a thing to be expected, but only those who suffer from it can tell how it isolates the sufferer, and how the still alert and active mind is withdrawn into itself and of necessity lives a life apart—on a plane other than the one which still attracts him from the outside.

My Father was welcomed freely in his new home, and the hospitality of neighbours was extended liberally to him. But he could not "find himself" in his new surroundings. He had never entered into general society alone, and his solitary position in a crowd of strangers was irksome in the extreme. It was his nature to be self-effacing and he would willingly have overcome his disinclination if by so doing he had given happiness to others: but his youngest unmarried daughter was then too young for society—a mere girl-school, who had never known anything but school-girl pleasures and companionship—and her elder sister was a widow who preferred retirement. He found it impossible to accept hospitality that he could not adequately return. It was a new view of things, to which he would never have become reconciled. He made the effort, and faced one large dinner-party alone, but it was enough!

Many blamed him for this. Old friends and comrades would fain have had him with them attending levees and introducing himself, in the status he had acquired, to a wider outside-circle in the greater world of the English capital; but his "comparative values" were different from theirs. It is beyond contradiction that the man who declines altogether to advertize himself, or even to keep himself in view of the powers that be, quickly slides into a forgotten corner. He might easily have become Genl. Sir Frederick Young, K.C.B.: in fact this distinction was within his reach but he preferred not to grasp it.

He rode and drove and took great interest in all outdoor occupations. There was some farm-land attached to his holding; and his growing crops, his grazing cattle, and all country interests filled his time. He was happy, merry, and cheerful, and always thinking of others more than of himself. Always, friends or relatives were his guests, but there can be little doubt that he must have missed his spacious life of old, and particularly the frequent intercourse with his military confrères whose lives and careers had followed the lines of his own past. In his study, when day was done and lamps were lit, he carefully read the daily papers and followed the march of time across the world, where old furrows were being ploughed over, and familiar aspects disappearing. More particularly he followed with intense anxiety the fortunes of the country that had been his home for so many years; and side by side with the politics of the day he must have seen visions and dreamed dreams of the great men he had known in the past.

But in all the letters which he wrote during that time and which have been preserved he never speaks of himself. When he visits relations or friends it is of them—their place, and their interests—that he speaks, never of "I", except in the *Te Deum Laudamus* which his heart always sang through the heaviest trials and the best pleasures. He never voiced regrets or murmured of changes. Beauty in all forms appealed to him, and he loved Nature—the changing seasons: the growing crops: autumn maturity, and spring flowers. There was one gate on which he used to lean at evening-time. It looked over a sloping meadow, and behind it the sun set and lit the clouds with Irish sunset-colours; the soft breeze touched him; he could hear the birds' "goodnight," and the merry voices of his children and grandchildren would sometimes reach him from the croquet-ground: but who that has lived long and grown old can doubt that at such times he heard other voices, and remembered other scenes? With his ever-prevailing consciousness that his "God was in heaven and all was right with the world" submission was his law, and with hope he looked into the Unknown beyond the narrow limit of earthly life. But that was the self that no one ever saw. Outwardly he had the brightest face, the cheeriest greeting for old or young, or rich or poor; a quick response to the mirth and laughter of the young; a ready sympathy for the old and suffering; he was beloved and revered by all who came in contact with him, and the star of Home to the absent throughout the years. But this description is not of a day, or of an hour, when he first began his life as a country-gentleman. It embraces the summed-up memories of the detached periods of my brief visits. I wish to portray his beautiful personality there in the dear home, unchanged and tried, a safe refuge and comfort as I always found him, when the waves of change and unrest guided me into harbour for a little space.

After my Father left me at Dinapore my husband's regiment, the 44th N.I., was stationary until the spring of 1856, when it was ordered to Agra. Jack—my husband—had bought the camp-equipage of my uncle, Colonel Bird, and I had my own carriage and riding-horse in which to cover the marches, so that I was considered to be very well-prepared for the journey as not many subalterns' wives possessed these luxuries. My carriage was a park-phaeton—a much more graceful-looking conveyance than what is now called a victoria—and we had a very handsome pair to draw it, a bay and a gray. On the day of the start Jack, after seeing the regiment off and completing his duties, had leave to remain and drive out with me, in the cool of the afternoon, to the first camping-ground. A large party assembled to see us start, and it really was a sort of triumphal exit. But it is the unlooked for climax to that proud scene that makes me give a sketch of my first march under all those glowing conditions!

We lost our way. We were timed to arrive at sunset or shortly after, but a night of stars set in and the darkness that comes before moonrise made our way more difficult. It was not a good road on which we found ourselves. At last the moon rose clear and bright and sailed up in the deep sky, which in all eastern countries is not a blue limit, as with us, but just unfathomed space; and by the help of her light we reached the difficult part of our journey which should have been accomplished in broad daylight. This was nothing less than crossing the wide Ganges River! On approaching its banks it was a shock to find that we had missed the ford, where our servants were waiting with a large ferry-boat to assist our crossing. Somehow, by dint of shouting and calling, we got a small ferry-boat used for small conveyances such as *ekhas*, and for cattle. What is a ferry-boat on an Indian river? It is a wide, flat-bottomed craft with no bulwarks: there is a man to steer and another man with a paddle. This was the only available thing to take us across a broad, swiftly-flowing river with eddies and currents disturbing its surface. This thing had to convey the carriage, two horses, two syces or grooms, Jack and myself, the *ayah* and her bundles, besides the ferry-man and his assistant. I can only indicate its size by saying that it was just wide enough to take the carriage allowing a few inches on either side of the wheels; the length was more convenient than the breadth. There was standing-room in front for the horses and grooms, and at the back for the coachman and Jack. I do not remember where the *ayah* went, but I do remember that I had to sit in that perilously-placed carriage.

I have said before that I am a coward. The horses with their nose-bags and their grooms went first, and accepted the situation quietly, then came the carriage with me inside in silent terror. On the opposite bank —which seemed miles and miles away—a fire was burning; a kind of beacon-light it seemed to me. And then we began to move. I thought that of course we should make straight for the bank and the friendly fire, but it was not so; we were in the power of the Ganges River, and a rapid current was bearing us down the stream further and further from our destination. The horrible clear moon looked down upon us in repellent indifference. But—*worse had to come!*

In mid-stream, as we sped along on the rushing water, the grey mare kicked herself over-board. There was no room for those standing behind the carriage to come past to the front. The *syce*, the wonderful *syce*, clinging to the reins and whatever he could grasp, fell flat on his face, and leaning over—at imminent risk—coaxed and comforted and encouraged his charge as she swam alongside. Every now and then she made a plunge and a scramble and tried to get her forelegs on the deck, and when she did so the ferry-boat tilted, and it seemed as if we must all slide off into the deep, dark, swift water. I think I must have gone through more than the experience of the drowning man. I know I thought of all those I loved who were far away with the solid earth beneath their feet, and—added to that—was the agony of suspense for the beautiful mare and for the brave man who was risking his life to save her! Oh! that cold, hard moon! Inwardly I vowed that should I ever leave India behind me, nothing should induce me to come back. . . . . I came back five times.

At long last the struggling mare touched land and her brave guardian jumped ashore to join her. The passage was over. Search-parties from the camp found us, and the curtain falls.

I would not wish to repeat this experiment; and though time softens all things I recall it as the most awesome of all my many experiences.

In May, 1857, the smouldering unrest in India reached its climax. At Meerut one Sunday morning the Great Mutiny broke out. Before I continue my story of personal experience in this great catastrophe I would like to emphasize a few facts in relation to it. And first: in these days ignorant persons use the term Anglo-Indians as meaning something that they call *below par*, whereas they really speak of an indispensable portion of the backbone of the British Commonwealth. In the same way I have heard people speak of "The inglorious story of Agra." They were not there. It is true that the first false steps of elderly men in a panic so utterly threw things out of gear that many suffered, as only brave men can suffer, when they realized that it was too late for action. But these sufferings were what the brave alone can experience. Self-repression and steady discipline require more true courage than many an impetuous rush to victory.

In 1857 most of those men holding high position in the country were more than elderly and were worn out by long years in a trying climate. They were lulled by security through a period of unbroken peace—years spent in plenty and in lazy luxury amid gay companionship and surroundings, with no daily fretting cares as in the mother country (for things went easily in that Elysium of grand old John Company). They were not endowed with the health and active vigour needed in this sudden emergency. This position added greatly to the difficulty which juniors serving under them had to meet and overcome, as it were in a day! When the military authority in Agra proved utterly inefficient—*as it did*—the whole onus of the situation was thrown on the civil rulers. Under the exceptional circumstances this was most unfortunate, as the man who held the reins and had the undoubted capacity to act in this sudden emergency was in very bad health at the time and often so ill that it was impossible to place urgent questions before him. It was not a matter for surprise, therefore, that trouble arose. Statesmen, rulers and even understudies cannot be made to order on the moment. We were cut off from communication, action was needed imperatively, appeal was impossible.

Military measures—essential to the situation—collapsed, and the one man who might well have filled the vacancy was so handicapped by bodily suffering—and at the most trying season of the year—that this episode became *what it was but never ought to have been*.

The sweeping condemnation, also, of sepoys, native soldiers and servants, was, and is, a great mistake. I give the true story of regiments that never mutinied, though driven into temptation, and the opportunity given them by mistaken rulers. If a *plébiscite* could have been taken in Agra Fort among the crowds of refugees who had run in for shelter from all the places round about, I know a large majority would have spoken in grateful terms of the fidelity of their own households. That was the general rule; and the story of the son of Lord Ulick Brown—afterwards Lord Sligo—had innumerable counterparts all over the disturbed area. Moreover, we must never forget in recounting our heroic deeds that the main defence (*i.e.*, at the Bailey Guard Gate) of the Residency at Lucknow was carried out by the sepoys of the 13th Native Infantry and their brave officers. What that defence was no one can understand save those who saw the ruined walls as they were left (before the beautiful creepers and shrubs had thrown a veil over them) and heard the story from those who had been through the great experience.

In those old days—and indeed for many years after—there was an institution in all cantonments called "The Coffee Shop." After parades and morning inspections and other duties were over, men used to assemble here, collect news, arrange sports and pastimes—and gossip! No women attended these gatherings, but so far as the propagation of scandal and "good stories" went they were not missed, for the work flourished without their help. So far as I can remember there were no daily papers; but long thin strips with telegrams and news of sorts appeared at the coffee-shops; and when the man returned to his household, if he was a married man, he brought the latest intelligence.

Of course at that moment all were eager to get news. We never knew how soon we ourselves might not be mixed up with events of the day. Women who were intimate, or were neighbours, generally visited each other after the morning ride or walk, to exchange information, or *on dits*, on the one absorbing topic. It is strange but true that I do not remember any of them being nervous or afraid.

It was the beginning of my fifth season in the hottest climate of that part of India, and it had been arranged that I should spend the summer in the Hills. Preparations had commenced, carriage and horses had been sold, and I was to begin my tour by paying a visit to an old friend whose husband, a civilian, was stationed at Shahjahanpur. But on the eve of starting I received a wire to say her father-in-law had died and they were obliged to go home at once. This altered our plans, very happily for me—and for them. Otherwise my visit would have had a sad finality. On leaving Church one Sunday morning the European community at Shahjahanpur was attacked and all were murdered.

One day my husband came back from the coffee-shop in the civil lines. I was always expecting something to happen, for I knew my own feelings, and therefore realized what strong men must feel. He looked shy and confused and turned very red when I asked "What news ?" He said : "Oh ! Mr. Harvey (the commissioner) is talking of going out with a small party to keep communications open with Delhi." And then he stopped. I said : "Oh !" and waited for more. Silence.

"When does Mr. Harvey start ?"

"Almost immediately." I knew there was more to come, so I said : "Out with it boldly—you have volunteered to accompany him as interpreter." He looked at me in amaze ; "How did you know ?" and I said in reply : "Because it is what I would have done myself." He was much relieved that the fact was known and accepted, and preparation could be taken in hand.

Mr. Harvey was an old friend of my Father. He was a very pleasant and agreeable man and I had seen much of him since my arrival at Agra. Everything that was a necessity was packed as closely as possible. Jack was to take his riding-horse and of course his *syce* Shunker—brave old Shunker!" If there is a heaven for the faithful he is there—though he did not enter his Valhalla for many years!

I decided to remain in my own house. Mr. Harvey left me the use of his carriage and horses, and directed the coachman to come to me every day for orders.

After Jack had started, however, I was forcibly removed from my anchorage. My kind friends, Captain and Mrs. Harris, would not hear of my remaining alone in my bungalow as it was on the verge of the cantonment, and carried me off to their own house in the military lines. Next morning I drove back to the bungalow just to pack up and arrange things, as everyone advised me to stay with my friends in safety, if there *was* safety anywhere.

I had sent a message to the lines for the pay-*havildar* to meet me, as I wanted money. He came, and other native officers with him. I had no fear. I implicitly trusted them, as they assured me of their fidelity and inveighed against the *neemukharam*, or renegades. The pay-*havildar* was a fine, tall man in the grenadier-company of a very fine regiment. I spent some time in talking to them. My native landlord came; and I paid the house-rent. My faithful guard remained beside me, helping as they could in the arrangements I was making, and never ceasing to regret the absence of the Sahib, "who could understand what they said." All my possessions were moved into two *go-downs*, as they were called—square rooms built of bricks and mortar with fire-proof roofs. I had packed all my most cherished possessions that I could not carry about with me in two large Bareilly boxes, including (alas !) a large bundle of valuable French lace that had belonged to my grandmother. The piano—a beautiful grand square that my Father had given me—I sent to Capt. Harris's bungalow.

The last place I inspected was Jack's dressing-room and office combined, from which I thought he had taken everything he wanted ; but, on looking round, I saw the pigeon-holes of his writing-table stuffed with papers, and many loose letters lying about ; so I concluded that in the excitement of the moment he had overlooked his private affairs. I called for a large bathing-towel and tied up and carried away every document I found. It was lucky I did so, as it saved many hundreds of rupees. Among them were things they called " step accounts." I do not understand and cannot explain their mechanism, but, some time after this, the bank on the authority of a man who shall be nameless—a brother-officer—demanded certain large payments. One letter in reply was to this effect :—

" Dear——,

" The Bank on your authority has been writing to me. You are seemingly unaware that my wife saved all my papers including step accounts, which are in my possession."

He heard no more about it.

During this time almost every night fires would break out in the bazaars and the lines, and while the sepoys were there they did much towards subduing them. Every officer slept in his uniform with his sword beside him—that is if he slept at all. Directly the alarm was given Captain Harris, as did all others, went straight to the burning locality.

On the wall of one of the rooms was an ornamental display of weapons brought home after the Santhal war; armed with these Mrs. Harris and I walked up and down the verandah, the boy in his cot close at hand. Under a tree in the compound stood the buggy and horse ready-harnessed, and our instructions were to be prepared to get in with the child, and drive straight across country to the artillery-lines. I do not think in the excitement of the moment that we thought of fear. We were intensely on the alert to act at once if necessary, and get the child—that was the first thought—into safety. But often since then, in sheltered security, I have shuddered at the thought of those long-past scenes, and the possible fate that threatened us so nearly. The spectacle we watched: the blazing barracks: the smoke: the shouts: the little black figures moving about, standing out against the leaping lights: the frightened servants crouching round us: no one knowing what was happening! At any moment the message telling us to flee on our risky journey might come. It is a horrible picture to recall, but at the time I did not realize it, and, if I tell the truth, my cowardly instinct was far more aroused by the fear of having to be driven across country by my dear friend Jeanie Harris, in whose driving powers I felt no confidence—and in a buggy! Of all man-made conveyances the one I most disliked to the end of my Indian career was a buggy.

And then the nerves of the civil and military old heads required some panacea, and they determined to pull themselves together and disband the two native infantry regiments. Loyally and without demur—recognizing the actions of their comrades throughout the country—they laid down their arms, asserting to their own officers that they now considered themselves as on *chowkadary* work, and were determined to stand fast. But nerves in high quarters were still requiring treatment, and a cruel—and, I must say it, cowardly—order was issued that at once the men of the 44th and 67th N.I. were to take two months leave and go to their homes. They protested in a body—and their arguments were sound: they had no arms, no ammunition; if they could do no good, they were fairly powerless to do evil—and they could guard the cantonments and their inhabitants from the *budmashes* in the district who were common thieves and murderers, out for loot. I saw and heard old men who had grown grey in service in the crowds that came to Captain Harris's bungalow where he had his office. I saw the tears in their eyes, and heard their plea: "Home? What home? Our home is with the Regiment—we have no other."

I had retained all my servants and once, when I drove down to my bungalow, because I wanted to pay their wages, and to take a look round, it was considered very risky; and at the request of some true friends I promised it should be the last time. On my return-drive the carriage was stopped and surrounded by men of the Regiment, many of them carrying their bundles—as was their wont—on sticks across their shoulders, and with their leave-certificates carefully wrapped and tucked into their *kummerbunds*. They all had one cry: "We want to stay and guard the cantonment." "Oh! why did the Sahib go away? So few Sahibs understand us."

I do not know if the tears found their way to my eyes; I was so young I think they must have done so. I know they were in my heart and rise there even now. Never have I shared in so pathetic a scene. It was with difficulty that I continued on my way.

Of course many will say (many do say): "How could we trust them when daily facts were proving they could not be trusted?" I pass no sentence; I only record experiences. I have mentioned that two sepoy regiments assuredly never failed to keep faith with us, but as assuredly we failed to keep our faith with them!

They were ordered out of Agra.

I know for a fact that many returned as soon as the roads were clear with their certificates fully attested—they were neither compensated nor reinstated.

During this time the fires continued as usual, and as long as any men remained in the lines they gave their loyal help; but afterwards the whole anxiety and responsibility was left on the officers and men who remained in the deserted cantonment to guard property, women, and children. This state of things could not last, but one more brilliant idea scintillated from the brain of the moving machinery. The order was issued that all women and children were to sleep in the Fort, going in at evening and coming back again in the morning. For their accommodation tents were put up on the parade-ground in the Fort.

Now everyone who has lived during and after the Great War has a right to know what is meant by—a public muddle. Well, as I have said once or twice, this is not a history of politics. It is simple experience. The civil and military cantonments of Agra must have occupied a large area, thickly-populated with officials and their families—officials of every grade, mostly married men with families and furnished houses—many of them one, two, or more miles from the Fort. It was quite the end of June, when the hot season comes to a climax, and the familiar description applies that there is only a sheet of foreign paper between the ground on which Agra stands and the infernal regions.

The most stifling moments of the day come after sunset, when even the stir of the hot wind dies down and leaves an oppressive stillness like the hot air from a blast-furnace. Imagine then this procession within a radius of two or three miles. Every sort of conveyance, every gradation in colour of humanity, from dark bronze to pure white women and children, invalids and sufferers. The men who escorted them had to leave them to their own resources, and hurry back to their deserted homes to return again in the morning, and repeat this weary ordeal from day to day. No servants were allowed—in a country and climate where women are trained never to lift their hands if they can help it. The road inwards from the gate of the Fort was hard and rough and very steep. Under the circumstances Captain Harris was obliged to use his buggy to carry his wife, and child, and an *extra member of his household* at the time. While he, in mercy to his beast, had to walk up that grilling ascent to the parade-ground. It drove me to action. I wrote to my friend Henry Prinsep, Mr. Colvin's A.D.C., a letter meant for his chief to read in which I explained that I was alone, as my husband was with Mr. Harvey, and could only obey the daily order by greatly inconveniencing the kind friends who were looking after me in my husband's absence. Might I remain in the Fort ?"

I received permission, as a *great secret*.

I took nice, airy rooms in a sergeant's bungalow and moved in with my personal baggage and three servants, thus saving my beloved books and relieving my kind host from a heavy tax on his goodness.

CHAPTER XVI

A Memorable Day and Night

"I cannot but remember such things were."

This must have been about the 1st or 2nd of July. Then suddenly the scene changed once more. A rumour came that a party of mutineers with guns was approaching. Hurried and secret orders were circulated that the unhappy crowd that took their journey to the Fort on that evening must take with them all the necessaries for a prolonged visit; and that the men who escorted their families were to remain with them, as they would be wanted. But it was to be done *as secretly* as possible. This was on the 4th July. Of course my kind friends came direct to share my rooms, and how delighted I was to have them! That night every square yard of shelter became a dwelling-place. No words can describe the confusion, or tell what nooks and corners were greedily seized upon and appropriated: numbers slept out in the open. They were not allowed the use of the tents on the parade-ground. Of course at the moment it was "everyone for himself and the——." I need not conclude the sentence. Every gunshed was a dwelling-house, every door-porch and archway had a bed, and impossible corners were curtained in for privacy, to give a little sense of decency to women and children. Before the night closed in most of us realized that, when the next dawn broke, the men would have gone to join the troops in the cantonments, and would move out with them against the enemy.

It can well be understood there was little sleep that night, and how, in silent terror, in hopeless discomfort and sense of loss, that miserable community greeted the dawn.

In the darkness that comes before the dawn every available man and boy of the whole community had silently left that crowded fortress to join the soldiers and civilians outside the walls, leaving behind their wives and mothers and children in bodily discomfort and plunged in mental misery and doubt. And surely no sun has ever risen to light up stranger groups of pale, stricken women and helpless children, and cowering forms of faithful servants dumb with terror. Jeanie Harris and I and Captain Paton, the Fort adjutant (and the only moving male upon the scene), spent the waiting hours of that day upon the ramparts, looking towards that place whence the distant sounds of action came. In the Fort was a strange silence.

This was the 5th of July, 1857. When I dare to recall the memory of that day that stands out from all other days in a long life it rises before me like a phantom through the mists of sixty-seven years—a time detached from ordinary time, a period of nervous strain and unwonted mental vibrations when the body *was not*, every sense being concentrated on one point. The blazing sun poured down upon us, and the fierce wind that dries the world rushed round us—unheeded: the sky of steel, the scorching heat that was reflected from every surface of that unprotected rampart, had no existence for our bodily consciousness.

Now I ask: was it I? living I? And the answer comes: The girl who lived through that summer day in the furnace-heat of that rampart-wall died long ago. It is her ghost that returns—that is all. In that truth I realize the magic power of vivid memory that can restore the living ghost to its broken, worn-out frame, renewing the old energy, courage and pain—yes, pain—as for a brief moment I face that strange world and am young again!

As we watched through the hours of that day, taking no note of time, we realized as in a dream that only an unprotected gateway was between us and the moving multitude thronging the city streets that lay beyond. Only those who know the market streets of an eastern city, and can picture what they would be like in times of turbulence can really understand the situation. As the sun lowered and shadows grew longer, that threatening murmur outside the walls grew louder, and, increasing like a rising storm at sea, more fully arrested our consciousness. And then—we suddenly came back to real life, roused by a woman's voice that said: "Our men are retreating; we are badly beaten."

In the abrupt awaking caused by these words there was no smallest element of fear. On the contrary, it roused the spirit of the race, and we felt as if single-handed we could face any foe. But we could not believe the words that fell upon our ears, so our pent-up excitement took the form of vehement anathemas on the wretched *Krani* who had brought the tidings, and threats of awful consequences to follow if the poor woman dared to spread such a report. Alas! in a measure it was true. *Not beaten*—our brave, fighting men were not beaten—but forced to retreat because those who should have known better had failed to give them the material (which was at hand) to enable them to carry on. Then the scene changed—there was stir and confusion and the sound of many voices. Our friends rushed to the Upper Fort to reassure us to some extent. Their faces hardly seemed the faces we knew. The draughts of cold water were gladly given and received—their lips were parched, their eyes strained and bloodshot, and on their cuffs and facings were fresh, dreadful stains that spoke too eloquently of what had been. Scarcely were words exchanged, for it was no time to linger and there was much to do—and suffer.

The tents on the parade-ground were given to the soldiers. The noble mosque with its hard, marble floor became a hospital—without beds! Some were comforted and some were desolate; but events were so crowded and sorrowful that nothing took a natural course.

To retrace the progress of that day until far past midnight I must tell the whole story as it eventually became known to us.

When our small band left the cantonment before daybreak, they found the enemy (including some mutineers with guns, and reinforced by outlying miscreants of all kinds), with such arms and ammunition as they had been able to annex, sheltered in a village some five or six miles from Agra, but our force had no definite idea of its strength or composition.

Our force comprised one small battery and one European regiment raised not long before and consisting chiefly of young soldiers newly-recruited who had chosen to remain in India on the departure of their regiments for home; there were also a few well-seasoned soldiers who had preferred India to England. The contingent, which would have been called Irregulars in times of organization (and may, indeed, be called so by historians to this day), was really only a scratch-collection of all sorts of brave men under no special command, but all bent on doing their best (from perhaps different grades of motives) under very exceptional and trying circumstances.

One thing of importance was overlooked in the

hurry of the moment! The blame did not lie with the gallant combatants. All authority had been resigned into civil hands. No runners were provided to keep open the communications; no transport arranged for to convey ammunition, if required, from the ample stores in hand.

The enemy, as I said, was concealed and sheltered by the walls and buildings of this village. I do not correctly know its name; I have always called it *Bhora* for a reason I will explain hereafter. I cannot describe all that happened. I only know that early in the action it became clear that the firing from their sheltered stronghold was so frequent and so well-directed that our regiment was ordered to lie on its face *en masse;* and once there (those who should have controlled the action exhibited considerable feebleness) the order was not given to advance and meet the adversary! It was here that most of the casualties happened. The battery worked hard, and its brave and beloved Commander was killed.

We are accustomed to the curtness of the British officers' descriptions, and so I record from observations made afterwards about "the battle." "It was chiefly 'potting.'"

One real soldier I know was there (though not holding any post of authority; he was on leave I think) who strongly urged the desirability of advancing and taking the village. But his remonstrances were unavailing.

At length the firing became less and beautifully less.

The rebels had exhausted their ammunition—and *so had we!*

Long afterwards a very clever picture was shown to me. It was drawn by Captain G———, R.E., and called

"THE BATTLE OF BHORA."

In the centre was a broken wall, and on one side, with his back to it, a dejected soldier looking into an empty cartridge-pouch; on the other side was a native on the run, with his head wrapped up in his chudder, and the ends flying behind him as he scuttled off. This is my faint image of a pencil-sketch on a scrap of paper.

For many a long day the discussion was: what the alternative might have been, but was not!

No doubt the battle of Bhora would not have appeared as one of Creasy's *Decisive Battles*, but, if the broken and flying column had been pursued with fresh relays of the abundant ammunition at hand backed by that dogged and inalienable resolve that cries out in the British soldier to retrieve a set-back, the outlook would have changed, and that poor, fatal day would not have had so miserable an ending.

But all the British were ordered into the Fort! All natives, even servants, were refused admission, and the gates were closed. The civil and military cantonments containing all our household goods were left unprotected. Agra was under civil rule.

And now I must add a few words: call it my "In Memoriam." Great records exist of brave men and noble deeds—of the self-sacrifice and devotion on the ridge at Delhi, and in the Hindu Rao post, and of the calm endurance and fortitude of men and women at Lucknow. But there is no laurel-crown for Agra! And yet—if those who know will weigh the balance fairly—will they not realize the deeds that are not recorded, nor written large, in the pages of history? Think of the acute and helpless suffering of those burning to "do and dare," in full consciousness of power, who yet had to bow to a rule they must endure, and which, for the sake of discipline they must not set the example of ignoring: think of the caged and helpless passion for action that—frustrated—was far harder to endure than the exhilaration of facing death in glorious sacrifice. That night and many that followed it were living torture to brave men. How truly Lucifer said "to be weak is to be suffering." It is the acme of bitterness. If you have no laurel for Agra, give cypress for slain aspirations, dead opportunities, and wounded *espirit de corps*. This is the true story of Agra, looked at from the soldiers' point of view, on the spot.

That night was also spent on the ramparts not only by three solitary watchers, but by crowds of helpless people who beheld their houses and properties in flames and heard the discordant roars of an unarmed rabble gloating in robbery and destruction—their joy slightly mitigated by the fact that there was no one to murder. Assuredly the wild beasts had left their den!

Remember that only the previous day these householders had been suddenly taken from their homes with only as much of their personal necessaries as they could carry; and remember what that means when you recall the contents of a family-household and the treasures it holds—treasures, not in money-value, but beyond what money can buy and not to be replaced. Fervently I hoped against hope that those stone *go-downs* of mine might escape, but as a matter of fact my strained emotions were exhausted and in abeyance after that terrible day. And who can count the mental moods in which those lookers-on contemplated the scene of destruction and watched their possessions turning into smouldering ashes before their eyes! One man—an artillery-officer—disobeyed orders. He got the range of his house, and as the shouting and scrambling mob approached he sent one ball straight through the building. *His house and possessions were left in safety!* This fact suggests an unanswerable argument. Captain and Mrs. Harris and I were not so fortunate. I had been able to bring all my things from the bungalow into my rooms in the Fort, but the beautiful piano my Father had given me was in the cantonment. Over and over again I had asked that it might be sheltered in the Fort, but in vain. Though I argued that in an extremity it might be made into firewood, the answer was that it would make "people fancy we were afraid." Of course we were afraid and the people knew it! That night its doom was sealed—my music's too. The latter included manuscript-music of untold value to me, dating back tens and tens of years before I was born, and with it was an authenticated (so my grandparent's said) manuscript-copy of Napoleon's own dream-book, with the code by which he worked it (some wonderful combination of numbers I cannot now recall). In the debris weeks afterwards two songs were found torn out of their books and strangely untouched, "Annie Laurie" and "Rowan Tree": I have them now. And the notes and wires of my piano were also there, not stolen and carried away but broken into little, little pieces and scattered over the road—not one ivory note intact.

For two or three days this orgy was allowed to continue. Then it became patent that it was very inconvenient to do without servants and with much care some were admitted. But all did not wish to return to the service from which they had been thrust out. I am afraid that some of us had a selfish pleasure in seeing magnates, who had helped to work the machinery of this disaster, obliged to work for themselves and their families in the dreadful heat ; fetching water from the distant lower regions where the wells were located, and doing other domestic drudgery.

I cannot remember dates but, very soon after the gates (now carefully guarded) were opened, detached parties of refugees would arrive—men, women, and children, with just the clothes they stood in. Few of those who were inside the walls had any superfluity to give in help ! Of course my rooms were shared with the kind hosts who had been so good to me, and we were, comparatively, in clover for the moment. Then one terrible, scorching morning news came that the ladies and children from Gwalior had reached the outmost bungalow in the European military lines and were sheltering there, destitute and starving. Their escort, from whom they had suffered much—a sulky and disorderly mob—had to their great relief left them. Too exhausted and almost too naked to move they were waiting to be brought into the Fort. I cannot remember how many sufferers there were. Many had seen their husbands shot down before their eyes, and three babies had been born *en route*. All owed their safety to one woman ; her name is entered on no dispatches ; she received no medals or honour or rewards ; but she was great and wonderful as the most renowned of heroes. She faced and cowed their unwilling and defiant escort. She commanded by her personality and inborn courage ; and all those women whose lives she had saved spoke of her with tears in their eyes. It could not be that they ever forgot her ? But no halo rests upon her name, except in that record which can never be effaced and which is far beyond this changing scene. The three infants born on the dreadful road and their mothers owed their lives to her ; she divested herself of all she wore to meet their wants, the climate fortunately helping her; and when they reached the deserted bungalow in what had once been a military cantonment she was still commandant and guard, with the coarse chudder of a peasant-woman for her sole garment! She was a beautiful woman—tall and graceful with long fair hair; and she had been the toasted débutante of a London season; and her picture still graces some long-forgotten "book of beauty." I do not remember her maiden-name, but, when I knew her in that strange, far-away crowd which is now just a misty picture in which there are very few out-standing personalities, she was:

MRS. DUGALD CAMPBELL.

THE AGRA BELLE: 1857

I refrain from mentioning names so far as possible but this one should be proclaimed from the housetops. I have a sketch of her which I reproduce as "The Agra Belle."

With an empty wardrobe and no possibility of going shopping, she had purchased from an Eurasian refugee the first crinoline ever brought to India! She was wearing it and, far from the world of fashions, it struck all beholders as a dreadful monstrosity, but it undoubtedly filled up a blank.

Of course Jeanie Harris and I were busy all that morning in making our own space as small as possible so as to take in some poor wanderers. Finally she and the boy and I shared two small rooms. The sitting-room was made as comfortable as possible under the very unfavourable circumstances, and became the dwelling-place of a mother and three children, the youngest of whom was one of the new babies. The mother was the daughter-in-law of one of our most famous generals in the Sikh War. Our dining-room became a sort of mess-room, where odd members of the community who had no homes were catered for. Captain Harris (who had found a bell-tent for himself) and Dr. Lacy, the kind, good friend of everyone, were the Presidents of this Club.

Before long things seemed to settle down in a wonderful way. We became familiarized with the strange aspect of the Fort, where every corner, crevice and archway, was a dwelling-house—the gunsheds were like a city-suburb where people called on each other! And some even made a semblance of entertaining their friends. The marble courts of the palace were thickly tenanted, and the mirrors looked down on groups of men in every sort of costume and colour, for the white man had no choice and none could consult a tailor!

In the evenings the band would play on the parade-ground, and children would run about and grown-ups promenade, as in days of peace. The whole community waited for tidings of the fall of Delhi. All this time we were our own prisoners, and no one was allowed to leave the Fort.

CHAPTER XVII

The Gallant Ninth Lancers to the Rescue

"Remembrance—saddening o'er each brow."

In the meanwhile the party that had left Agra with Jack as interpreter (and he filled every other post that could be assigned to him) was moving about, now near, now far. The object was to keep open the line of communication and bring in, or send in, to Agra the earliest news of the fall of Delhi. Of course it was well-known that we had large forces from the north concentrating on that point. The few previous years of comparative quiet had obsessed our comfortable rulers with the general impression that we had only to come and be seen in order to conquer. It took some time to correct this flaw in their prevision.

So this small party was waiting about: it consisted of civilians and men in civil employ: there were two military men, one whom circumstances had thrown into the group, and one who had willingly volunteered his services under the original rule, building castles in the air as to joining the new army. The original idea had been to go on to Delhi, under the impression that their mere presence in the district would suffice to clear the road! But whatever attractions, possibilities, and temptations presented themselves, under the circumstances Jack was loyally bound to remain at the post he had undertaken, and it became a most purposeless and perilous task. Of course the head-men and small chiefs of the district, not knowing definitely on which side their bread was buttered, supplied escorts for the Commissioner's party, but from the first these were not trustworthy; they began by being insolent; then they deserted without warning; and finally they openly mutinied and, after doing as much harm as they could, joined their brothers-in-arms. At last our people were just a band of refugees fleeing from one place to another, in great difficulties, often barely escaping with their lives, and losing all they possessed. They were in want of food and clothes and medicines, sometimes receiving what we sent out, sometimes having everything looted by wandering miscreants (who were too strong to be followed and captured), or by small, thieving groups who took all they could get and ran away. Letters came in occasionally, and my kind friend the A.D.C. arranged both to receive and to send out, when it was possible, my letters. These, folded about an inch square and hidden in the corners of some runner's waist-band or *kummerbund* or *puggaree*, and written with poor ink on any available scrap of paper, are now stained and impossible to decipher. Often the runner bringing them had to swim through deep streams or be soaked through and through by tropical rains. I give the few extracts I can decipher; they will briefly explain the dreadful life our friends had to lead.

> "We have been a long round since I wrote and yet we are almost in the same place again. It is very humiliating that so many Europeans should have had to turn tail.
>
> "We have to retreat on the banks of the Jumna, N—— having bolted with the escort. At a rumour that one of the *sowars* had been shot, and that a party of mutineers were on the move and going to attack us, the whole of our party bolted! and

G—— and I were left with six Irregulars to do the fighting, and even when we proved the rumour was false it was very hard to collect the scattered band.

"No news from Delhi. I believe I am to ride in with dispatches when the news comes.

"We are all right at present. A heavy storm has saved us from the descent of a new party of mutineers; I was out on detachment duty the last time, and found on my return that our men had risen; I have lost everything to my name: indeed we have only what we stood in—and put on native garb when our clothes are washed. 'Honeysuckle' (*my dear, beautiful grey arab*) carried me fifty-six miles when on the run without grub or water.

"And what *I* think more wonderful still—the gallant *syce* Shunker kept up with them the whole way! He died in our service long after he was past work."

At the beginning of August sickness broke out, and in a local cessation of activities this futile expedition was given up and they all returned to Agra, to wait—with the rest of the community—many weary weeks for the fall of Delhi.

The next sketch in this shifting story was the 10th October, 1857.

After news of the victory every one was on the *qui vive* and the seeds of courage began to put forth a few leaves. People were allowed to go outside the Fort-gates, proceeding with much caution, and to walk or drive about in the immediate neighbourhood. Some brave Eurasians even got permission to look up their ruined homes and arrange for restoration. Otherwise things remained as they were.

Then with joy the news was received that a large column under Colonel Greathead was coming down to Agra; that the district would be cleared and resume its normal aspect; and the Fort would gradually disgorge its teeming population. But this desired state of things was not yet, as there was a rumour that the Gwalior contingent with its guns and cavalry was on the prowl.

I do not think our intelligence-department was ever very good until the Great War shook it into being. At this time it was a little inactive. Lt. Jenkins of the late 44th N.I., always on the look-out for active exercise, was ordered to go with an orderly and find and mark out the next encamping ground which might be required by Greathead's force when he moved out of Agra in pursuit of this rumoured contingent. On the eve of starting to carry out this arrangement the order was countermanded, as being premature before Greathead's requirements were known!

This, probably, was an escape for Mr. Jenkins and his orderly, but it was a grand mistake on the part of the authorities as it might have revealed to them the fact that the enemy had progressed rather far on their prowl!

So, on the morning of the 10th October the weary column came in, after many forced marches over devastated places. Men and beasts were longing for rest and food. After camp-duties were discharged all officers who could be spared got leave to visit the Fort, and see their friends, exchange news, and be welcomed and fêted. And all the men who had no duties rushed out of the Fort to gladden their eyes with the sight of their eagerly expected comrades. Hospitality was being freely extended within and without the walls. We were sitting at breakfast, and at last life seemed worth living, when—thud

—thud—thud—the roar of cannon broke the stillness !

There was not time to question why ? or whence ?

Those in the Fort rushed off without a word to join the camp : those who found themselves outside were frantic to return to cover. Shouts and most emphatic language in English and the vernacular filled the air as, on the narrow bridge before the gate, the opposing crowds met and obstructed each other, and for a while pandemonium reigned !

The camp was pitched on a very large *maidan* : the ruined cantonments surrounded it : and on one side was the church and the old churchyard, where for decades of years the bodies of our English dead had been laid to rest. No one had been near it for many months, and the grass had grown tall and thick above the graves—as grass *can* grow after the rains in India. The day before the Gwalior contingent, undetected, had camped upon that very ground the authorities had decided that it was too premature to inspect ! In the darkness of the night the enemy's men and horses and guns had stolen round quietly, entered the churchyard from the further side, and silently hidden themselves in the long grass. All unsuspected in this close proximity, hostile eyes watched every movement in Greathead's camp ; saw all the precautions laid aside, in a fancied security ; saw the weary men divested of arms and accoutrements, bent only on food and rest ; saw the guns unlimbered, the horses tethered—with the bliss of nose-bags and free limbs ; watched the officers gaily cantering away, and the welcome sense of rest and well-earned laziness taking possession of the strong men before them. Their looked-for opportunity had arrived. Thud—thud—thud—the hidden guns gave voice only a few hundred yards away ! It was a chance—one in ten thousand ; no doubt these ambushed warriors pictured to themselves in anticipation the scene of a conquered field.

> " The rider distorted and pale,
> The tents all silent, the banners alone,
> The lances unlifted, the trumpets unblown,"

But the men facing this cunning movement were equal to the occasion. It was the 9th Lancers who faced the enemy and bore the brunt of their attack. Their quick recovery from the outburst spread the example all along the lines in every direction. The gallant regiment, with the young subaltern on duty, led the way, all unmounted and unaccoutred as they were; every unit in that weary column was in active movement; it did not take long to capture the nearest guns and put the fear of the *feringhee* into the gunners. The enemy fled along the road by which they had come; and short, sharp measures organized that pursuit that finished the day.

Few of the enemy retraced the path they had so confidently followed twenty-four hours previously, and of those who escaped—without arms, without guns, without any rallying insignia—the harmless remnant just vanished. This was the day that Dighton Probyn won his Victoria Cross, and yet another hero is mentioned in some lines I am going to quote written by one of the many who are content to be heroes without any name, and are fully rewarded by the consciousness that the enemy is not.

I forget who showed me the lines. I copied them and I need not say they were written by an Irish bard!

Agra 1857 10th October

> Oh! comrades all if you'll attend
> You'll hear how Pandy met his end.
> 'Tis now well known he did intend
> To murder all the babes in Agra,

But Greathead's column that morn crossed
  The bridge of boats, and as they passed
Were loudly cheered by numerous hosts
  Who had little love for Pandy.

Our camp was pitched and all was quiet
  When some of these fanatics hove in sight,
But two of our chaps put out the lights
  Of those daring Mungal Pandies.
We were attacked when tired, 'tis true—
  But what will not bold Britons do?
Some hundreds on that day we slew
  Of the murdering, rebel Pandies.

The Lancers caught it rather hot
  For they were first upon the spot.
Brave French there met a soldier's death
  While charging Mungal Pandy.
Bold Jones in the bridle arm was shot
  But still he charged a numerous lot,
And twenty other wounds he got
  From a murderous lot of Pandies.

Our Artillery soon began to roar
  As shot and shell they sent galore,
Which made the Pandies curse the hour
  They came to fight *Feringhees*.
Our gallant Light Bobs soon were there
  And the cornfields did quickly clear.
Down came the steel! Hurrah! Three cheers!
  Then to —— went lots of Pandies.

The Sikhs they fought as in days of yore
  But our General gave them credit for more!
Though he never named a British Corps
  In one of his Dispatches.
So the Pandies hooked it in despair
  But were closely followed in the rear,
By dashing fellows who will not spare
  One baby-murdering Pandy.

We followed them ten miles or more ;
  Such a licking they never got before ;
We took 13 guns, their camp and store
  Away from Mungal Pandy.
We got some loot and then "Retreat"
  Was sounded as 'twas getting late.
Our killed and wounded were twenty-eight
  That day we beat the Pandies.

And now in Agra we've arrived,
  Thank God so many of us are alive,
And the ladies are trying to relieve
  Our comrades who are wounded.
Then may the dears who do attend
  Our wounded never want a friend ;
And by St. Patrick we'll defend
  The darlings from the Pandies.—*A Private.*

This is not high-class poetry! But there is something in it that speaks directly to that something that makes "the whole world kin."

I am glad to add my testimony to the fact that "bold Jones" who had "twenty other wounds," and whose life was long despaired of, ultimately recovered and, much scarred and beaten about (with one eye cut out by a sabre-wound, and I think only one arm left), lived a soldier's life for many a day and died at a goodly age—a retired Colonel. A bit of luck for him that he was on the spot that day! His men always spoke of him as a hero.

No regiment in the service has a better right to judge of heroes—than the 9th Lancers!

Until the end of the year detachments were hard at work all round, clearing up the district and freeing it from insurgent-parties who still lingered here and there. It was horrible work burning down the villages—destroying the wasps' nests as it were, but it was necessary before the poor victims of these cruel marauders could safely return to their homes and cultivate their lands. Sometimes, no doubt, the innocent suffered with the guilty, but the people anxious for the old *régime* of security did their best to help those who were trying to restore order. Of course in all this Jack was an eager sharer, but never again under civil command! He had a fine old soldier to serve under, and the work, although it was inglorious enough, was done thoroughly—fully and generously, but without too much caution when the inevitable had to be faced. At the same time it was fairly safe except for the ever-present risk of all warfare. But they did not carry their lives in their hands or have to turn their back on the foe they were out to subdue.

Letters now began to come in from home, and my dear Father strongly urged that I should be sent home at once, and the point he emphasized was this—that it would leave Jack free to do a soldier's first duty without being in any way hampered by family responsibilities. This was also my view, and I determined to act upon it in spite of all the difficulties that had to be overcome. The most important of these was that no women were allowed to travel down country. They say that where there is a will there is a way, and I had the good fortune to find it. The manner of my journey from Agra was unique. I never quite realized *how* unique until long years after, when I read a passage in a book which I will quote presently. This will form my best sketch, as a matter of history that is not likely to recur in the experience of my descendants.

CHAPTER XVIII

"Stole Away." Heroes and Home

In sooth—it seems a hundred years!

Now that the central parts of India had been fairly well controlled and were becoming habitable once more, and Lucknow had been relieved, the next great undertaking was to conquer Oudh. An immense force was being drawn together, and fighting was going on unceasingly to clear the ground for a winter campaign.

Enormous supplies of stores for the use of Sir Colin Campbell's great army had to be collected from those districts that had not been laid waste; they had to be ultimately conveyed to Cawnpore and Allahabad, and were to start from Agra, where the details of transit could be arranged under the protection of the Fort and a fitting escort provided. My impression of facts is this: the old Indian commissariat-department had been scrapped by (I think) Lord Dalhousie, and a new department was developing. To save money and to nip in the bud an extensive system of bribery and corruption, officers and responsible men were now arranging the contract with native merchants, and the huge preparation for a mixed assemblage of native and European troops was being carried out. This necessitated a wide knowledge—something beyond the mere vernacular. Intuition and a little watchful intelligence brought me to the conclusion that Jack was considered to be rather a useful person. He had linguistic attainments as well as the reputation of being a good accountant. And so it seemed a secret in the coming future (a secret not totally unsuspected by him) that he might be wanted with the growing convoy. If so—I should again be at a loose end.

I made up my mind to go with the convoy.

Of course the idea was too preposterous to express and I had to think it all out very carefully. First of all I used diplomatic means to extort the fact from Jack that he would start with the convoy, then that he might go all the way. "Of course," he said: "just for that short time you could share a house with some one in Agra, until the roads were clear and you could go to Calcutta *en route* for home."

"No thank you," I said to my little self, but not aloud! I was like the parrot: I did not talk much, but I thought a great deal. I was, however, bound to mention my plans to my friend Jeanie Harris as she also had arrangements to make. She was very kind and did not laugh me to scorn, but tried to impress upon me that the thing was impossible as *no woman was allowed to travel*. A general was expected to superintend matters. Without a word to anybody I simply bearded the lion in his den! He was rather surprised. I was twenty-three, but a little creature, and did not look my age. I said:

"I want leave to travel down with the convoy and go home."

He was very kind and gentls, but impressed the old argument, "*ladies were not allowed to travel:* he had no voice in the matter: why had I come to him?" Then for the first time I unfolded my whole plan. In doing so I had to disclose the facts that I had a husband, an English maid and a baby!! Poor man, he was appalled.

It is not necessary to enter into the details of my battle to get my own way, but my logic and arguments prevailed—on these conditions: I must guarantee absolute secrecy and my husband's consent. Of course that was easy enough. I had one good card to play. Jack was as anxious to get me home as I was to go. He fully realized, as Father did, that family responsibilities would be a great weight on his shoulders, and would considerably hamper him in his absorbing work under exceptional circumstances. The plan I had sketched out was quite feasible considering the position he would occupy; and the men under his control—also in their self-interest—would do whatever he told them.

I had been fortunate enough to secure a helpful companion. She was called maid or nurse, but she soon became a trusted friend. She was a brave, strong, cheery woman. She did not wish to remain with the family whom she had accompanied to India, and, indeed, had been so anxious to escape from her position that, earlier in the year, she had married a very young soldier in the 3rd Europeans. He was young and lonely, and she wanted an active interest in life. They were married on the very day when everyone was ordered into the Fort, and she left him at the church-door, to return to the family.

She never saw him again. He was killed on that fatal 5th July.

She heard through my friend Dr. Lacy that I wanted someone to help me, and we soon came to terms. And now I will explain my plan.

I had decided that I would travel in a conveyance called a Bombay *shigram*. It was a species of covered cart which could be provided with good shelter from the sun. It was wide and quite capable of being well-cushioned, and it was drawn by bullocks, like all the other carts. Jack with his army of subordinates could be sure of good bullocks and a good driver. My own trusted *kitmatgar* who had never left me all through the troubled days was to sit beside the driver, and when the time for a rest and a short halt came those two men would take the *shigram* to the Sahib's tent, back it in, and Kitty and I would get out and stretch our legs, have a good bath and change of linen, and also a good dinner, and get back into our conveyance with the baby, so as to be ready to start long before daylight to take our inconspicuous way in the noisy, dusty crowd.

This plan was carried out. Of course we had our ups and downs and some sleepless nights, when we could hear the guns thunder and the fusillade not far off, and had nothing to do but keep still until the next halt to hear all about it. When it could be managed without attracting attention Jack would come to the tent, but of course he was playing the rôle of bachelor, and was honorary member of one or two messes. This tent was supposed to be his office-tent, and was guarded. My plan was therefore a great success—we were moving on!

And here, to give an accurate picture, I must speak of Miss Taylor's *Memoirs* of her father, Sir Alex. Taylor, R.E., with all the information it contains in extract from her father's notes of his eventful life and experiences. I read it with much interest. I knew him and his wife very well, and remember Miss Taylor as a beautiful baby, *the* beautiful baby in a world of babies. The book contains an interesting account of the long struggle before Delhi while we, in the Fort of Agra, were looking for their help: it mentions scores of men whom I knew in after years and danced with and rode with under the glorious, peaceful sunshine of primitive Muree and Rawal Pindi, never thinking of them then as heroes—there were so many—with brilliant records accomplished and more to come in the future! I want to quote here particularly her father's description of the convoy I am speaking of. It is strange that, until I read it, I never fully realized the real romance of my journey. I never spoke of it —it would have been breaking my bond—until the lapse of time had opened the seal and no one lived who could be punished for breach of orders! Gen. Sir Alexander Taylor says:

> "Early in December Genl. Seaton was put in charge of this convoy with directions to see it safely to its destination and *en passant* to pacify the country on either side of the road down which it had to travel. No easy task, for the province was studded with forts and fortified villages and overrun by large bodies of mutineers and rebels, while the convoy to be defended was 'immense.' 'An enormous thing,' Sir Alex. Taylor calls it, writing from Manipur. 'Just picture to yourselves,' he adds, '3,400 Haekeries from Aligarh, 2,000 from Agra, total 5,400 irrespective of camels, etc. These would occupy 31 miles of road in single file.'
>
> "General Seaton disposed of his difficulty of defending this long mileage of stores, enveloped in a cloud of dust and the hubbub of a moving multitude of men and beasts, by depositing it under the shelter of guns: and it was only after he had engaged the enemy to the front, and closed and occupied the road that he allowed the mammoth train to roll forward."

This was the convoy. I and my companions were inside and had no definite idea of our surroundings, but Sir Alexander's description fills well the blanks, and my readers must think of us as a tiny speck in the "multitude of men and beasts"—an item of stores!

Captain Harris had been appointed cantonment-magistrate. He had taken as good a bungalow as could be obtained among the ruins, and I was with them. We all moved out of the Fort together, I think on the 31st December. So I spent New Year's Day with my old friends. Very late into the night she and I sat over the wood-fire talking of past and future. After dark the *shigram* had been brought to the door, and while the household was wrapped in sleep Kitty had arranged the interior of our future dwelling for the coming strange weeks. Jack and Captain Harris did not show themselves—it was not in the play! Very silently—as silently as it was possible to move a driver and his bullocks—we joined the convoy leaving Agra on the morning of January 2nd 1858. Of course I had not failed to impress upon Jack that once we were off in the *shigram* we should be a *helpless item of stores*, and have no more responsibility, but be on his hands; so he, poor fellow, had a heavy burden on his shoulders. But, as I said, all went fairly well; no one grumbled, and I blessed the Fates that had sent me Kitty.

The next incident on our strange way is worth noting. One morning I woke up to find Kitty in great excitement, sitting up and peeping out of the window at her side of the van. She said, "I was just going to wake you; there is no sign of the convoy; we are quite alone and going over ground that has no road. There are all sorts of things lying about—they must have been fighting here."

It can easily be imagined that I, too, sat up and peeped out of my window in alarm. To my great relief I saw a horseman riding beside the van. On recognizing a very valued and trusty friend I opened the little glazed frame and put out my head. I began to question, but he put his finger to his lips and shook his head, so with much relief I closed my casement, and reassured the anxious Kitty. We were quite safe and only had to keep quiet. But to be prepared for emergencies we preened our feathers and awaited development. Our furtive glances soon revealed the fact that we were entering a large camp, and then as usual our van was backed into a tent doorway, and a kind voice said, "Come out and have *chota hazree*."

We were in Sir Colin Campbell's camp at Futteyghur!!

Major T—— had learnt from Jack that I was there and all the story. He said the convoy was halted at a dreadful place, and that, as he could not endure the thought of my being in the middle of it, he had brought me to his own tent, which he would give up to me for the day, and that he would take every precaution that my secret should be kept safe. "But," he added, "come out now, and have *chota hazree*."

"You dear, kind man," I said, "we are here, but all our clothes are with the convoy!"

"Never mind," he answered, "I'll bring my big *choga*." So Kitty, in her dressing-wrap over her nightdress, got out of the van; and he brought his *choga*, and she held it up before the doors, just as in old days a bathing-woman at the seaside held up the dry towel to replace one's dripping dress that had been toying with the waves—and with the joyful and elastic spirit of youth my little person disappeared in the *choga's* ample folds, and we enjoyed his welcome hospitality. Of course we had much to say to each other. Major T—— had been on my Father's staff at Dinapore.

After reconnoitring to be sure I could see without being seen, he brought up some splendid Highlanders, to make me "feel quite safe," he said.

After that day of liberty and rest, when it was quite

dark, my carriage came up to the tent; and we again took our places in the crowd and proceeded on our way. He risked a good deal by that kind act. Had it reached the Chief's ears that women had spent a day in his sacred camp, there would have been no future career for my tried and trusty friend! And I am sure to this day if anyone who was in that camp in, I suppose, February, 1858 (but I never remember dates) were living now (and some may be), he would not believe my story. But it is true.

I am very hazy about the continuation of the pilgrimage. I know I had some obstacles to overcome and uncomfortable episodes to endure, but eventually I found myself and my little band once more in a *dak gharri* on the Grand Trunk Road, with horses this time. I started from Benares. I have the old paper of the route, rather ancient and crumpled, with Jack's instructions written outside. I believe I was the first woman after the departure of the Lucknow ladies to travel on the road. I think they mostly went by river-steamer.

It is rather interesting to read the memorandum.

> "The train leaves Raneegunge at 10.12. Go to Rose's Hotel. Fare is 1st class R.11.15.6, 2nd Class R.5.10.9. Give the coachman in charge 8 annas each—nothing to *syces*. At the bungalows if you do not stay over two hours, you must (I think) give 1 rupee for accommodation, your food here being extra. You must not stop more than one hour daily—so as to ensure being at Raneegunge early on Saturday morning. Where there is a post-office send me word how you are faring."

The first two days from Benares I was warned to be on guard, and never to let the coachmen parley with road-side friends. I had a revolver but I was afraid of it, and found *backsheesh* my best weapon. I only remember making one threat—which I am thankful to say ended in brave words! After that we continually met parties of marching troops going up-country, and my reception by the soldiers was enthusiastic. I never shook so many hands before or since. God bless them all!

In Calcutta my father-in-law was waiting to take me home. I also met some dear friends. I write their *In Memoriams* here.

First there was Mrs. Aitken, wife of the brave defender of the Bailey Guard Gate, Lucknow. He was R. C. Moncrieff Aitken, V.C., 13th N.I. (another regiment that holds a proud place in the annals of the Indian Army). His name and deeds are prominent in heroes' history. She was my very dear friend all her life long, a beautiful woman without guile. Calm and brave, without self-consciousness, fulfilling every duty in life. I have heard it said that when Lucknow was relieved and the women and children walked out of that Bailey Guard Gateway—still under fire—her white dress looked quite fresh and tidy, and her beautiful face with its brave calm smile made her surrounding guards adore her. Then came Etienne St. George, captain in the 1st Bengal Fusiliers; he held an appointment in Calcutta when the mutiny broke out. At this time he had obtained leave and was about to rejoin his regiment on the war-path. At the taking of Lucknow, in a square from which one window had rifle-men doing havoc among our men, he asked volunteers to follow him and take the room from the miscreants. His own account was:

"Half-way across I felt as if someone had given me a punch in my side; and I remember no more

—no pain, or suffering—until I recovered consciousness long after, and found the doctors treating me as a raree-show."

The fact was that a bullet had passed right through his liver! He was reported mortally wounded; but he did not die. He used to say that, as he was the only Englishman on record who had ever survived such a wound, his convalescence was the hardest part of his mishap, for all the doctors wanted to know why he was alive! He lived long—a beautiful and loyal life—always a hero.

And then there was Mr. Cubitt, who had been Col. Aitken's right-hand man all through that troubled defence. He was the last man in the retreat from Chinkut. He brought in three wounded men, one on the saddle before him, and one on each stirrup-iron, thus saving from cruel and ruthless death three fine men who recovered and did good work through the siege. He was quite a lad then, modest and unassuming. He never talked of this deed as anything out of the common. He told me the first man he tried to save was a soldier on a wall who had been shot in both legs but was waiting with his weapon charged for an opportunity to do some sure reprisals! He was indignant at the idea of flight—almost angry with this "boy" who wanted to help him away. "Me," he said, "me turn my back on those d——d niggers? I'll die first."

And he did.

At a dinner-party in London afterwards Mr. Cubitt happened to be near some great man whom he did not know but who, struck by his modest way of recounting experiences (which at that time everyone wanted to know), found out his name and regiment, and Colonel Aitken was asked about him. The result was a V.C., given to him by Queen Victoria's own hands! And Colonel Aitken told me that, even if that act of valour had never been performed, he richly deserved his reward for all his acts of self-denial in every way. In the time when rations were short he would surreptitiously make over his share to some one whom he thought required it more. He was another life-long friend. I missed them all when they took precedence of me in—the Great Adventure.

It was my great privilege at a later date—twenty-four years later—to walk with Colonel Cubitt over the scenes of the great siege, and so to realize in an exceptional way what the circumstances—so calmly and unemotionally recorded—must have been. Two incidents I will relate here: they are of those that unavoidably rouse the feeling of humility in the face of that—Unknown—that surrounds frail humanity.

The great defence of the Bailey Guard Gateway calls for some imagination in those who visualize it truly, as it was at the time of the siege. To the left of the Gateway there was a bungalow with the ordinary low, thatched roof and surrounded by a pillared verandah. A few feet in front on the side that looked outwards was a broken four-foot wall; and with only the breadth of the road between were tall, native houses of irregular form with odds and ends of balconies and flat roofs and narrow windows. These bristled with fire-arms of sorts and often with expert marksmen. When I saw the place, however, the houses had been levelled and the greater part of the ground covered with grass and planted. Standing in the verandah of the broken bungalow in the peaceful beauty of a lovely evening it was difficult to bring before me the scene as it *had* been, and yet the incident recorded above compelled me to re-create the true picture. Standing beside the ruined pillar Colonel Cubitt said;

"Just here I had a *chilumchee* (brass basin) on its stand, and every morning when roused from my rest to go on duty my first act was to plunge my face and head into the water. One morning, moved by a sudden impulse, I lifted the *chilumchee*, stand and all, and placed it against the inner wall. While my head was in the water a round shot came through the pillar, breaking it (as you see), and passing through the very space where my head would have been under the usual circumstances."

When we were standing on a flat roof with a far outlook, Colonel Cubitt explained to me that it had been a most important picket. Sentries on duty and officers in charge had to be constantly relieved, and as numbers decreased it grew more and more difficult. One night he was on duty; he had just finished his round and was making for his *charpoy* (camp-bed) when he noticed a young sentry with wan, white face and heavy eyes. "You look done up," he said, "give me your musket for a while and lie down on my bed." "He did so,"——the narrator paused; a look of intense feeling came over his face and I saw the memory was too much for him. There was a short silence. "Poor lad! In five minutes more, his body lay, dead—on the place where *my* body should have been."

Very many years afterwards, when peace was well-established, a member of the old garrison said to one of the leaders of that great rebellion:

"Explain to me this thing that has often made me wonder. Why when in your thousands you came on that Bailey Guard Gate with its frail defence did you pause and retreat? You must have known that with one swoop your numbers could have annihilated that small force and that then the whole place would have been in your hands?"

"Sahib," the man said, "it was this: when the forefront of our advance came on the Gate and saw nothing to resist them but a few Englishmen standing calm, quiet, and unafraid in front of their little band of Sepoys, no one durst approach them, for they thought some secret power—known only to their enemies—lay between them. They thought of mines and other devices; otherwise they could not understand the calm, unflinching attitude of the men who faced us. We did not know—we feared the Unknown."

Spiritualists talk of the "aura" that emanates from the good man. So in this case the great and true defence of this small group was the aura of courage that struck back the foe.

But I knew nothing of these things when in 1858 Mr. Cubitt was a fellow-passenger on our voyage home from Calcutta, and earned my deep gratitude. Many times he nearly allowed his gold watch to be eaten by the baby when she found the voyage irksome and wished to say so.

On our way we touched at Galle where, to their deep disgust, my brother's regiment, the 50th ("the Fighting Half-hundred"), had been halted on their way to India. I had not seen Charlie since 1849-50.

We continued the journey overland—that is by Marseilles—through France. This is an experience that has certainly been improved upon. The small space and most uncomfortable crowding have given way to every convenience.

A female passenger did her best on that occasion to make it worse. She was *en route* from Australia and called herself Lady D. My father-in-law was fairly well-known and he had sailed with the Captain before, so at once on starting from Calcutta he, the Captain, gave me the place of honour at table with my father-in-law on his other side. After dinner had commenced the first day, Lady D. sailed in. She was a woman of stout proportions though not tall—the smallest part of her was her nose which was not exactly tip-tilted but carried with a disdainful, assertive air! She stopped in the doorway; the Captain was busy carving (they carved at table in the good old days) and could not leave his post, but he said to the steward: "There is a lady standing, find a good place for her quickly." With some repressed mirth the steward came back: "The lady says she's a lady of title, and her only place is at your right hand." Confusion. I felt rather puzzled as to what I should do, but the Captain did not hesitate.

"Tell the lady," he said, "that we have no rules of precedence on board. I like having my friends near me."

Lady D. in the doorway assumed a still more stiff Napoleonic attitude.

"She says, Sir, she will not take any other place. She'll have her meals on deck."

"That as she pleases," said the Captain, and sure enough she kept her proud resolve and lay in wait for a reprisal!

On the Marseilles boat there was only one cabin for the ladies, and here the offended dignitary tried to revenge herself. Having left the baby in a happy sleep with Kitty beside her, I had been enjoying a beautiful, calm Mediterranean-night on deck. I always relieved Kitty at a fixed hour. In the enjoyment of the moment I may have exceeded the usual time, but on arriving at the cabin-door I heard my infant giving tongue in bold protest. She was the only child on board. Kitty and the other ladies were wildly protesting, but the plump old lady with the assertive nose had locked the door and refused to deliver the key until she was ready for bed. I think my share of the music was playing the big drum outside the door! And then—the poor old girl had a most ignoble fall. The key fell down too. It was seized and I was admitted. I think Kitty annexed the key! On the way from Marseilles I had the happiness of a pleasant revenge. She saw my father-in-law was an expert traveller, so she followed our footsteps as regarded trains and hotels. At Lyons I found her in great trouble. She could not speak a word of the language and she had no French money to go on with. I was not a much better linguist myself, but Mr. Cubitt was brought to the front and we soon made her happy!

We reached Paris rather late in the evening the train (having experienced some delays) being long after its time, and we were tired and travel-stained and very hungry. My husband's married sister was in Paris, or rather at Versailles, for Colonel Beadle's people lived there and were known very well. According to instructions from my father-in-law they had taken an imposing suite of rooms at the Louvre Hotel, and everything was ready for our reception. We were received with some ceremony. The blessed baby was sound asleep. Orders were given that Kitty should have an ample repast served in her room in our suite, and, as the men were desperately hungry, my father-in-law suggested that I should use a dressing-room on the ground-floor, just to tidy myself, and that he and Mr. Cubitt should come for me and take me in to dinner. Will your imagination, my readers, be equal to visualizing the scene? After the destruction of shops and houses at Agra some one had gleaned from the ruins a dress-length of warm material of a Scotch plaid, very dark and quiet (black and green, a blue of sombre tint, and just tiny lines of red and yellow). A clever *dirsey* had made the skirt and plain, tight-fitting (very well-fitting) body, and in Calcutta I had invested in collar and cuffs of what was called "chicken work," which was in fact very superior *broderie anglaise*; as we approached the colder regions I had much appreciated my warm plaid; and I had plenty of changes of collars and sleeves or cuffs. I looked quite fresh and nice when we got into the train at Marseilles. But we had now spent the better part of three days and nights in a smoky train. Some inches of dust had settled on the dress: the cuffs and collar were black! I could only wash my face and hands and try to smooth my hair. My male companions did not look smart, but that merely meant they had come off a long journey. This was Paris—Paris in the time of Eugénie; and the Louvre was a very large and very fashionable hotel; and the magnificent dining-room was full of beautiful flowers and sparkling glass and silver, and brilliant toilettes and sheeny frocks! An elegant dancing-master sort of individual met us in the anteroom, and with many bows and scrapings assured the handsome old gentleman—who had engaged that excellent suite of rooms—that our places were marked and that our dinner should at once be served. I have said I was never shy; this time I came a little near it—sufficiently near to make me very uncomfortable! We were late. The greedy people had done eating and, feeling serene after good wine, were looking about them. Naturally I was the cynosure of every gaze with my smoothly-brushed hair, and my tightly-clinging plaid skirt, instead of the inevitable balloon! Dear Mr. Cubitt felt my confusion and he walked between me and the lookers-on when he could, and my one comfort and courage was my thought: "Poor things, if they only knew what a hero was walking beside me!" We had a very good dinner. I had never seen a French menu before and, being at the moment inclined to disdain everything French, I resented seeing my dear potatoes called *Maître d'Hotel* after the dancing-master who had given the brilliant lead into that assembly, to my poor, dusty, begrimed, little self!

I must have been an aggravating little thing. My one longing was to get home, and shopping never attracted me. I was taken to choose a silk dress which was to be my father-in-law's present. I made my choice in the first moment, but I remember seeing bales of silk taken down and spread out and patted and put in different lights: but I adhered to my first choice. Then came the dressmakers. Well they had one reiterated cry! But not flattery, nor any amount of cunning, could make me change my reply. They said:

"*Il faut porter une cage, mais—il le faut.*"

The stupid little English girl only said, "jamais." I left Paris without one.

And then in course of time we saw the white cliffs of old England. Mr. Cubitt and I stood side by side at the bulwark. We did not speak, but he felt—as I felt—the thoughts that were too much for utterance. How often we had known in far different scenes the thoughts of home, and the wonder whether we should ever again look upon the English shore.

My beloved Father came to meet me and very soon we were in the Green Isle and at home!

All the sisters were there and their children, and there was much baby-worship over the new arrival, aged about six months : but the real, honest thought of each in regarding the returned wanderer was: "Good gracious ! She hasn't a crinoline ! "

CHAPTER XIX

Over New Ground

"A murmur of waves from a distant shore."

I remained on what I may call furlough until October, 1859. A part of that time was spent in England, and while I was at home my dear Father was quite active and energetic. He spent some months of that summer in Jersey, and was so delighted with the beauty and fertility of the Channel Islands that he almost changed his dwelling-place. But all his people in Ireland dwelt so much on the inconvenience of the stormy winter-seas that would rage between them that he did not go far with his negotiations.

My husband had been employed very busily in the still active regions of India. He had been put into that branch of the service which still required able men, and had been posted to an upper grade, receiving the thanks of Government for his services ; and finally he was appointed to the charge of the large and growing station of Rawal Pindi in the Punjab, which was only one night's *dak* from our northernmost frontier at Peshawur. The climate for nearly seven months of the year was delightful, and for the very short hot-season (there was no doubt as to its being very hot) the beautiful hill-station of Murree was close at hand. It was just being initiated as a convalescent depôt, and new roads and new houses were rapidly growing up.

It seemed as if this appointment had been especially

designed for the renewal of Jack's Indian home and the return of his family. So it was settled that Kitty, the baby—now two years old—and I, should return to India in October, 1859. My father-in-law thought it advisable to try a new route, and made all necessary preparations for the voyage; while my dear Father, with unequalled generosity, saw me equipped with an abundant supply of everything to furnish the new home! All our old possessions, with very few exceptions, had gone to the Agra robbers, but he gave me plate and crockery to fill in all deficiencies, and another beautiful piano almost better than the first. And not only that—but he sent them all out, and we had nothing to pay for the transit! For many years I was greatly envied by the wives of generals and commissioners who had to depend on local sources which were all in their early infancy. In those days everything that one wanted—even positive necessaries—had to come direct from Parsee merchants in Bombay and Karachi. Beer was the staff of life in those days! It had to come up-country in large casks, and its arrival was an event. We were not pretentious yet, in those merry, primitive times. The family-man who had received a cask of beer and had omitted to ask a party of friends to celebrate the broaching of the cask before bottling its contents was—taboo! Invitations to dinner even among magnates had the note "R.S.V.P. Camp fashion," which meant that each individual's table-attendant was to bring knife, spoon, fork and plates. As each person had his kitmatgar, attendance was rather crowded, and—tell it not—if you happened to have nice things of your own, it was necessary to employ a detective on your staff to count over after a festival! As, thanks to Father's generosity, I never had to put "Camp fashion" on my invitations it was the more necessary to be sure that those attendants who came empty-handed returned in like manner. But I ought to arrive at Rawal Pindi before discussing it.

My father-in-law had selected this new route by which we were to leave the mail-boat at Bombay, take a steamer to Karachi, and then proceed up the Indus to Multan in a river-steamer. Judging from the map it seemed shorter and more convenient as we were travelling with a young child; but it was in fact untravelled as yet by ordinary passengers, and when it was too late to alter arrangements he found it impossible to estimate expenses exactly, so he gave me a circular-letter to his bank in Bombay instructing them to do all that was needful, and to give me every assistance.

So the three wanderers started once more, on 20th October, 1859. The "baby who never cried" (as an old friend used to call her) did not approve of leaving *terra firma*. When the paddles revolved and the great steamer trembled she knelt down to steady the floor with her two little hands, and cried out excitedly: "Tum, Titty, tum, the ground's moving." But even Kitty had no power to stop the wheel of destiny.

After emerging from the Red Sea we turned to our left and crossed the Indian Ocean to Bombay; three miles before you reach port you can smell the pungent odour of the East. It is not "spicy breezes," but scents and sandal-wood and something that is like nothing else—not disagreeable when far-off and in the fresh air, but you can have too much of it!

At Bombay agents and people from the bank came to meet me about my onward journey, and I received three severe shocks in quick succession.

(1) The steamer for Karachi left the next afternoon (it was now late in the day).

(2) The Karachi steamer was unfurnished, and I should have to provide bedding and all the necessary furniture for a three days' journey, as towels, etc., etc.

(3) There would be *no milk* or anything requisite for feeding a baby! Even for adults it was necessary to be supplied with tinned foods and even coffee, etc., as nothing was provided for English women or children—such not being expected, and the boats not being built for their accommodation.

It is hardly necessary to explain my state of mind. Even my brave Kitty was dumbfounded. One fact was clear: all those things had to be provided and put on board in less than twenty-four hours. But the big question that loomed above all was *milk*—that delicately-nurtured little two-year-old came before everything. I think it was the ship's doctor who in our despair suggested a goat. So that also had to be obtained; also its food; also its caretaker. The only comfort was that the money-question did not interfere, I was to have what I required, and you may be sure I did not count the cost! There were two British subalterns who were on the same route. God bless those English gentlemen. They were veritable guardian-angels to me. Their names were Fenwick and, I think, Glasgow. I have never seen them since. However, they wore themselves to thread-papers in rushing about, helping Kitty; while Kitty helped them in the purchasing-line; but *they* found the expert to select the goat and provide the fodder, and the man in charge. The bank-man paid the bills. And at last we were off! There was one other lady-passenger caught in the same toils as ourselves and equally miserable, except that she was alone and had no responsibility or care beyond herself.

Even if everything had gone right the component memories of this voyage would be worry—smells—cockroaches—and repulsive meals, with the veil of dirt over everything.

But it did not go all right.

This boat was a tub built in the year one, and fitted in her old age with a screw worked by steam, so she was called a steamer! I do not speak positively but I do not think there was much "white man" about the crew or the captain; however, I confess my memory does not visualize them: when we had been at sea for a day and a half we began congratulating ourselves that we were getting through our three days' torture, and then—a sudden commotion occurred!

We were letting-off steam at a great rate, and men were dashing here and there, climbing masts and pulling about ropes and cordage. The sailors spoke a language no one understood, but they made it pretty evident that our room was preferable to our company—so we left the deck and faced the new confusion below. After a short and awesome suspense my dear boys brought us news. The screw had become detached from the stern and was exploring the hull on its own account. There was no power on board either to lift it into position or cast it loose. The one resource was to sail the ship, and to that alternative the drawback was that no one knew much about sailing.

However, as this was made fairly easy by a calm sea and favourable winds, all might yet be well if the screw would be gentle in its demeanour and not knock a hole in the bottom. Meanwhile the screw loudly asserted its intention of being both rude and noisy. Its reiterated smacks on the stern just below our cabins were like rumblings of earthquake-shocks and most discomfitting.

Also, the unwonted delay *en route* necessitated our being put on rations, of which the only feature I recall was raspberry jam made of cockroaches. We learnt what it was to have a screw loose!

The other poor lady had very jumpy nerves, and directly I had fallen asleep at night—after an exhausting raid on uncooked cockroaches, slain in their scores by my slipper on the walls of my cabin—she would scream for me. Always the same cry:

"I know it has knocked a hole through the ship. Are we going to the bottom? Shall we all be drowned?"

I could only say, "I don't know, but I hope not! I don't think it is worse than usual."

"Oh! please, please call the captain!"

This went on every night and all day, only then the kind boys took her off my shoulders.

Fortunately the weather continued kind and calm until we got into the swell that they told me always plays about outside Karachi; there I had for the only time in my life a dim conception of what people call *mal de mer*.

I had been advised in Bombay not to try hotels in Karachi, but to go to the *dak bungalow*, which was near the starting-place of the Indus steamer. Mrs. M. went to friends, and the boys to the military camp near at hand. It was an intense relief to be alone and try to rest. This did not, however, come at once. Attracted by the dirty copper money called pice—which in an unguarded moment Kitty had left lying about—the baby, probably connecting it in her young mind with chocolate, promptly tried to swallow a handful! With a dash and valour that *I* could never have attained to, Kitty's long, skilful fingers at the first choking cry performed the operation of extracting the money—to the last farthing.

The horrid fright seemed to be the last straw in my accumulating burden. When Kitty had pacified the infant and between us we had soothed her to slumber, she turned her attention to me, and, while making all snug for a night's rest, she fixed me into a deck-chair in the verandah and told me to keep quiet!

It was a glorious night. Everything seemed for the moment to be at peace; and I was very weary and wandered to the borders of dreams—not sleep. In that pleasant wonderland I heard the fifes and drums, and then the last Post—the dear soldier-music that had been silent for nearly two years. A wave of feeling swept over me. I was lifted into some happy region and the space around me was filled with ghosts —but they would not stay at my call.

Again I was wideawake in a Karachi *dak bungalow*. . . .

I remember nothing of the transit, but once on board the Indus steamer it was temporary rest, and my elastic temperament soon recovered. The Indus steamer had an Englishman as captain and one or two white men under him. All was clean and comfortable. My two boy-protectors went all the way with us.

I do not remember where we stopped as regards the places *en route*, but I vividly remember how often we stopped where there were no "places"—but sand-banks in mid-stream! Indeed the ordinary routine was: steam ahead for one hour and go aground for six! Progress was slow—weary work for women, but good sport for the boys. They could always manage to get on shore and spend the time in shooting. They brought back all manner of birds with them, but chiefly I remember the black partridge. Some wings were cured for me, and I arrived at Rawal Pindi with one in my hat, and set a new fashion in the Punjab!

My husband met us at Multan.

The next scene was a *doolie*-journey through clouds of dust over *kutcha* (raw) roads until we crossed the famous ford over a narrow stream that could rise "like a hooded snake" with little warning, and established many a fatal record for man and beast.

Two friends awaited our arrival. As I reached the gate into our compound I put my head out of the *doolie* and called "Bob! Bob!" and in one moment a great black-and-tan bull-terrier leapt into the *doolie* and nearly annihilated me. My beloved old dog! He had been left at Agra until Jack had found a home. It was a veritable welcome! The other friend was the *syce* of whom I have spoken—Shunker. His fierce eyes under the heavy brows gleamed with pleasure, and his broad, unwonted smile as he bowed to my feet in repeated salutation without one word was as honest and expressive as Bob's had been.

This was Christmas Eve, 1859.

I spent four beautiful years at Rawal Pindi and Murree, then in its primitive loveliness. There were roads that were little more than goat-paths, primeval forests with their untrodden carpets of wild, scented violets, and graceful ferns; maiden-hair, both large and small; Solomon's Seal in size beyond compare with that which we know; mosses of all kinds; and beautiful winged creatures of every size and hue; distant snow-peaks; and sunsets that showed-up in the varying light the innumerable mountain-ranges that gradually rose between us and the unsullied heights.

This was very far from the snowy range of my youth, and my Father's young days: but still the world in some ways is small, and I met there an old man who with his wife led a sort of hermit-life at Murree, never leaving it even in winter. He told me he had known my Father, and now I recognize him to have been the young engineer De Bude who—helped by Dr. Royle—had improvised the battering-ram for the taking of Fort Kunjah (see p. 60). Of course I did not know it then. He liked to talk to me about what I had seen of the mutiny. He smiled at the panic that had prevailed in these remote regions.

"I felt we were all safe," he said, "but of course the women and children had to be comforted and guarded. My wife guarded me! While I slept like a log she sat over the fire with a poker and a Holy Book, ready to give the alarm."

The old man's day was done, but he had a son who trained and commanded the mule battery.

The Mule Battery!

There is not much of a triumphal sound in the words and not every one who reads them can measure the marvels they represent. I suppose most people have seen manœuvres at Aldershot and elsewhere and know the wonders of artillery-action on those occasions on the great smooth plain. Let their imaginations shift the scene to a mountainous, roadless region, with sudden descents and declivities having little more incline than the wall of a house; let them picture the swift climb of the mules, the unlimbering, placing in position, firing at the objective: and then the limbering-up, and the speedy descent that takes them from your view. Almost quicker than thought can follow they appear again on a further point standing-out against the sky-line!

I little thought, when sitting under a civilized lady's parasol on a quiet hill-side and watching the magic mimic-show, how soon Captain De Bude and his mules would be in the throes of real, wild hill-warfare with death and danger on every side. But so it was.

After a specially gay and festive season in the early autumn of 1863 orders were received in rapid succession: "join your regiment"; "proceed to the front"; all "without delay." And very soon the Murree Depot was cleared of its gay and gallant multitude and there was hardly a man left in Rawal Pindi.

One afternoon a note was brought to me.

"It does not matter what your engagements are, you must ride with me this evening. I have had my orders and go down the hill to-night."

It was from Captain Davidson of the 1st Punjabis.* We never met again.

Jack was ordered off in the very responsible command of his department. Gradually only the few men on local duty remained.

I stayed in Murree as long as possible. Part of my house at Rawal Pindi was occupied by Jack's successor. Arrangements were on foot for our return home, as the child's health seemed to indicate that her stay in India had been long enough.

It was a real grief to me to leave that beautiful place. The house that Jack had bought I had called "Peterville" after Peter Lumsden, who was its former owner.

My dear garden was full of English flowers raised from Sutton's seeds and holding their own in all the festive decorations. But these were at the time minor considerations, for our thoughts were in the mountain-passes before Umbeylah where many a gap had already been made in our circle of friends.

* See p. 251.

CHAPTER XX

UMBEYLAH: 1863

> "Days of old that shone
> Saw—what none shall see anon—
> When we gazed thereon.
> Gone!"

I waited at Rawal Pindi until the end of the campaign and Jack's return. He had much work to do before leaving India, and so could not accompany us, but I was glad to carry away with me the copy of the thanks of the Government which I quote, and the notice of his promotion.

"No. 51a.
"Adjutant General's Office, Hd. Qr. Camp,
"Peshawur, 8th January, 1866.

"To the OFFICER COMMANDING PESHAWUR DIVISION.

"SIR,

"I am directed by the Commander-in-Chief to request you will communicate to Capt. J. H. Jenkins, D.A.C. Genl., the congratulations of His Excellency on the very successful manner in which that officer conducted the arduous duties of his Office while employed with the Eusufzaie Field Force.

"Independent of the official reports that have reached Sir Hugh Rose respecting the commissariat arrangements of Capt. Jenkins every officer who has spoken to His Excellency on the subject has given the most unqualified testimony as to the admirable manner in which the troops of all ranks European and Native were, under very difficult circumstances provided uninterruptedly with rations of more than ordinary excellence throughout the recent operations.

"For this most important service to the Troops the Commander-in-Chief desires to offer his sincerest thanks to Capt. Jenkins—who is at the same time to be assured that His Excellency will not fail to bring his services on this occasion specially under the consideration of Government.

"I am, etc., etc.,
"D. M. STEWART, Col.,
"Deputy Adjutant General."

"I have great pleasure in forwarding this letter for the perusal of Capt. Jenkins who will be so good as to return it to the A.A. General.

"(Signed) JOHN GARVOCK,
"Major General."
(TRUE COPY.)

Attached to this official document was a little private note which personally enhances its value.

"MY DEAR JENKINS,

"I congratulate you old boy! A certain Brevet for you. It is some little compensation for all your hard work.

"I give the letter to Paddy Boileau to save the post so that the Memsahib may see it.

"Yours very sincerely,
"T. WRIGHT."

Just before leaving Rawal Pindi my dear friend and companion, Kitty, married a man worthy of her. He had seen much service and done good work. I place my memorial of him here. Shortly after this he won his well-merited commission; it was served on for many years, and he retired as a major. He and his wife lived happily, devoted to each other. They had a dear little home in the Isle of Wight with lovely roses in the garden. As long as I could move about, I used to pay them a visit every year, and one of the pictures in my collection of memories is of his upright, soldierly figure with the glad smile of welcome on his face and the beautiful white hair uncovered by his uplifted hat as he greeted me on the pier.

Kitty, however, did not leave me at once. Both she and her husband wanted to place us safe at home before arranging their own future.

So the three wanderers made another journey from the Punjab frontier to the old Irish home, still a bright and happy place of rest under the light of that personality that made it so dear. But before I continue I feel compelled to say a little more of the Umbeylah Pass and the Campaign in Eusufzaie.

It is all very unfamiliar to the present generation, but I am pleased to have in my possession a small *brochure*, written at the time by some one who is unknown to fame; although many whose names are mentioned are remembered still. And these reminiscences may fall into the hands of some who hold links of interest with the past. It is not a story told with blare of trumpets and loud acclaim. but, if great deeds of valour and self-sacrifice are the real crown of the human race, it is a story that introduces us to a kingly array of the "forgotten dead!"

The object of the campaign was to subdue hostile tribes who raided and devastated the peaceful valleys that were under our protection. In the effort to secure peace with as little sacrifice of life as possible, minor expeditions had been undertaken with fair results temporarily; but the enemy, growing more aggressive and greatly increasing in strength and power, rendered necessary those strong measures that alone can impress these hill-rebels who are as brave and dauntless as they are ruthless and cruel. And now many of them, since they have realized our motives and our power for good, have become our true and trusted soldiers.

I add a few extracts from

UMBEYLAH

A POEM BY LOUIS H. TUCKER.
DEDICATED TO THE BRAVE MEN WHO GUARD
OUR NORTH WEST FRONTIER,
1863.

The Advance.

October's eighteenth sun had not yet set
When the whole Force at Nowa Killa met.
A group conspicuous on a rising mound
Surveys the troops deploying on the ground.
Pause then, my Muse, a moment and declare
What gallant knot of men stands clustered there?
First, Neville Chamberlain whose cold grey eye
Experienced marks the columns passing by;
And at his right there stands of aspect mild
No less a personage than Colonel Wilde.
Whilst on his left we turn to look again
At Ross, the friend, the darling of his men;
And Alexander Taylor—known so well—
Before whose pluck and science Delhi fell
Has joined the Force, and now is standing there
With Tupper Carter, and with Tony Blair;
Whilst somewhat farther back, luxuriant down
Conceals the massive face of Buster Brown.

Amongst the Staff we recognize old Wright;
And little Allgood, painfully polite:
And Jenkins too, to whom we little know
How great a debt of gratitude we owe;
He softly greets us with his light blue eyes
And whispers one delicious word "Supplies."

Beyond all others it shall be my pride
To tell of those who nobly fighting died.
Of gallant Richmond who with dauntless breast
For days and nights defends the Eagle's nest:
Of Davidson who, when the others fly,
Alone remains within the crag to die:
Of Chapman who, himself when dying, bound
With tender hands a younger comrade's wound:
Of Clifford whose brave heart with ardour burned
To lead the charge from which he ne'er returned.

The next night Wilde and the Advanced Brigade
March to the entry of Soor-Kawa's glade.
About the break of day they reach the pass:
Here on this spot Wilde and his troops await—
Calmly expectant—the decrees of Fate.

Behind them see a most promiscuous mass
Of guns and soldiers filing through the pass;
Mules, camels, elephants, and cursing men
In dire confusion crowd and choke the glen.

The Reconnaissance.

"Explore the pass—descend into the plain—
Endeavour all intelligence to gain.
Avoid if possible the arduous fight
And see that you return to camp 'ere night!"
So spake Sir Neville! Alex Taylor then
Collects a small but gallant force of men.

A rugged road proclaims the Sappers' force
Made chiefly for the use of Probyn's Horse.
But think not then on that eventful day
That Probyn's Horse alone shall bear the fray.

One hundred glittering sabres of the Guides
There were of gallant troops there besides;
Of Foot—about six scores their orders take
With prompt obedience from Lieutenant Drake.
While Brownlow brought a party of his men,
I think amounting to some twelve score ten.
They reached the Chumba vale just as the sun—
Unerring watchman—marked the hour of One.
Here halt the Foot. . . . . . .
But Taylor never weary—scours the plain
Nor yet returns to Kagah till the sun
Descending warns him that the day is done.
But now with some anxiety they learn
That unopposed they may not now return.
For Bonair's Chieftain viewed the audacious feat
And now determines to cut off retreat.
Hundreds of warriors quit the Kotal mound
And lie in ambush on the broken ground.
Charge, Probyn, charge! oh! India's *beau sabreur*
Now shall that spear oft-stained in blood before
Lose its bright lustre drenched again in gore.
At furious pace his swarthy troopers ride
And on at headlong speed they madly go,
Hurl themselves recklessly upon the foe.

As the deep thunder peals its echoing knell
So hoarsely, wildly sounds their maddening yell.
'Tis but a moment—then is changed the sight—
The scattered foe betake themselves to flight.

'Ere this the last, faint, pencilled streak of light
Had left the heavens and faded from the sight.
One winged messenger of death, alas!
Strikes down poor Gillies helpless on the grass.
One muttered prayer, one stifled groan,
And all is o'er—his ransomed spirit flown!

The Right Defence.

Next morn the sick, the wounded, and the gear
That can be spared, are ordered to the rear.
The enemy are quiet but one sees
Their various standards floating in the breeze.

By these our skilled Commanders recognize
The Mudder Khail, and far famed Hussanzaies,
And Hindostanies known in frontier war,
Under the Standard of Moobarak Shah.
These with the Chuggerzai in force unite
To send a party to oppose our right.
Those Keyes commands—Keyes whose intrepid soul
Can combat foes, or angry friends control;
Keyes of the 1st Punjaubees*—he whose name
Shall live while India's sons aspire to fame;
Keyes famed for daring—let his praises ring
Till armed Calliope shall cease to sing!
With him are Pitcher, Davidson, and Hughes,
All men of gallant heart and sturdy thews.
The enemy at morning's early light
Take up a strong position on the right.
And Keyes by long experience taught
Calls upon Colonel Wilde for some support.
In the meantime, within his bosom rose
An ardent longing to attack his foes.
The strong desire he knows not how to quell
It seems to suit his Irish soul so well!
And so while Davidson attacks their flank
He storms the hill and climbs the slippery bank.
Unused to such a sharp, interpid fire
And quite outflanked the beaten foe retire;
From point to point they vanish from the view
And Keys with his two hundred men pursue.
At length our men a rugged summit gain
Which overlooks two hundred yards of plain;
Here they repose till from the camp arrive
Some British troops to keep the game alive.
And the 5th Goorkhas clothed in rifle green—
In action gallantly shall these behave,
Dauntless as lions, bloodthirsty as brave!
Short, sturdy little men as e'er were seen—
The guns of the Peshawur Mountain Train
Laden on mules the rugged summit gain:
Beneath their withering fire no foe can stand
And shot and shrapnel thin the Afghan band.
So, when at last the word to charge is given
The foe, like cattle from their pen are driven.

* Now Punjabis.

The author, though he feels the tragedy of all the surrounding scene which is so graphically described, expresses at intervals that light-hearted spirit that never quite deserts a British warrior even in extremity and though I am just picking out the passages that bring before us the men and their deeds I must give the proper tone to his narrative by an illustrative quotation :

The Eagle's Nest.

The man who weary goes to sleep best knows
The sweet refreshing influence of repose
If, in addition to being very beat,
He happens not to have a thing to eat,
Nor aught to drink—not even that good friend
His pipe its soothing influence to lend :
Should too the night be cold, as well as damp
And dark, and he have neither rug nor lamp :
If then his only pillow be his arms,
His lullaby incessant false alarms,
I think—but do not know if I am right—
That he, perhaps, may not enjoy the night.
As I lay weary, sprawling on the ground,
To my intense discomfiture I found
A comrade very restless in his place
Putting his booted feet upon my face !
In vain I shift and move, in vain protest,
He only mutters "Damn the Eagle's Nest" :
Though why he thus condemned it to perdition
Seeing it was the key to our position,
I can't conceive ; unless he augured ill
And prophesied a heavy butcher's bill ?
If such the case he certainly was right
For early morning ushered in the fight.
A steep and rocky knoll upon its crest
Displays the picquet* called the Eagle's Nest.
A breastwork runs around the Knoll which, when
Well filled, contains about one hundred men ;
And at its base a few large rocks behind
Some six score more sufficient shelter find.

* The writer spells this word picket and picquet indifferently, throughout.

Vaughan's picquet lies adjacent—Abbott there,
And brave De Bude with their guns repair.
A most determined charge the Afghans made
And though De Bude's guns upon them played
Audacious, fearless, onward still they pressed
And climbed the steep sides of the Eagle's nest.
Not less determined the resistance shown
By those behind that rugged wall of stone
Where lion-hearted Brownlow holds his own.
Half of the picquet *hors de combat* fall:
The rest undaunted still defend the wall.
Heroic deed! Here gallant Richmond stood:
Then fell his temples bathed in crimson blood:
Died as he lived—unflinching, undismayed,
Nor word, nor moan his dying lips essayed.
But as he fell, with failing strength he pressed
Beneath his coat, his Bible to his breast,
And trusting firmly on his faith's reality
Passed from this life to glorious Immortality.
Not unavenged, for, as the foe retreat
Young Clifford leads the charge with active feet;
His arm of vigour deals the sturdy thrust
And flying foemen bit the blood-stained dust.
Too far adventurous youth thy ardour leads!
Thy daring soul delights in doughty deeds.
No more, alas! shalt thou in life return.
Who love thee best in tears thy fate shall mourn.
No more thy light and ringing laugh shall cheer
Thy men, and drive away debasing fear,
But evermore thy home shall honoured be.
Richmond and thou, the souls of bravery——
——Had it not been for Beckett, brave and calm,
When Clifford fell his men had come to harm.
He, if report be not a wanton liar
Refused—in spite of orders—to retire,
And with a few men covered the retreat
And warded off disastrous defeat.
Although our left position bore the brunt
Of the attack a picquet on our front
Was driven in, and Drake while turning round
To leave the place received an awkward wound.
The Sergeant-Major, Cowling, who was near
Carried him on his shoulders to the rear—

A gallant deed whereby he saved his life
And bore him safely from the arduous strife.
So ends the day—the hard fought battle o'er—
Many have fallen who shall rise no more.

The Covering Party.

Three weeks had passed—as near as I can say—
And still the Afghan forces bar the way.
Sir Neville's soul, impetuous, ill could reck
So long, so fierce, so well sustained a check;
To Alex Taylor then his plans he shewed
"Forward's my motto—but I want a road."
"A road?" said Taylor, "very well, the Sikhs
Have done good service in the past three weeks.
They'll make your road, but I would pray you send
A party out, the workmen to defend."
Sir Neville turned and standing by his side
Was Harding, radiant with a warrior pride.
"Permit me, Chief," he said, "to take command.
I swear by Heaven," and here he raised his hand,
"To hold the post whatever may befall
Till you think fit to order my recall."
"Go, Harding, go—I'll send you a relief;
Till then be cautious, or you'll come to grief."
So spake the Chief, and Harding straightway flies
With hope and ardour flashing from his eyes.

Why Harding stayed can never now transpire,
After he got his orders to retire
Within his picquet? But we know he stayed
And the withdrawal of his men delayed
Till nearly dark, and under cloak of night
Retiring still maintained unequal fight.
First Murray fell, and Harding next a wound
Received, which stretched him prostrate on the ground.
In darkness and in flight no man dared stay
To help to bear the wounded man away.
And so they left him, and he lay and saw
His doom approach. . . . . . .
He nerved his arm and grasped his sword
For one last blow, then sank upon the plain
Never to see the light on earth again.

Among the dead is Dougal, who without
Obtaining leave had sallied out.
Among the wounded Oliphant we see;
And lying pale, yet gay, beneath a tree
Is gallant Wigram Ballye of the Guides—
An Afghan bullet past through both his sides
Had stretched him prone—but strength and pluck shall save
My noble school-mate from an early grave.
Long may he live—the ladies' favourite toast,
His regiment's darling, and the army's boast.

The Crag.

Among my readers doubtless some are not
Acquainted with the great Akound of Swat;
The country round his wards obey with fear
To far Bajoor and still more distant Dheer.
The Bonair Chiefs have called him to their aid:
He comes—and coming preaches a crusade.
Round him a hundred Standards flaunt, and hope
Cheers the brave followers of the Moslem Pope.
To them the Akound thus his words addressed:
"Fear not the guns, ye children of the Blessed."

* * *

On this the Afghans firmly calculate
And pay the penalty of tempting Fate.

* * *

Umbeylah annals now before me lie
Recording how The Crag was lost and won,
And the first words that meet my searching eye
Tell of the death of gallant Davidson—
'Twas then on Friday at the hour of ten
The Afghans made a vigourous attack
And though the picket held some eight score men
They all save one alone—were driven back.

I must insert a remark here. The author does not give the correct impression: they were not "driven back." A letter written to me by a mutual friend who was there says: "Davidson held the picquet with his own men, and through that night they had repulsed no fewer than fifteen assaults." In the morning a relief was sent consisting of British soldiers under the command of a subaltern. The first appearance of the fierce heads of the enemy over the slight defence struck terror into the heart of this young officer. He bolted—his men followed him and were in turn followed by the brave, loyal few who had so strenuously done their duty through the night. Davidson was left alone :

He stood—an army in himself—and tried
With prayers and threats the panic to allay.
If naught can stem the fast retreating tide
Of British heroes when they run away,
Say ! what more noble can the gods create
Than he who stands alone in danger's hour,
Defying death when Honour is at stake,
His only fear—the glorious fear of shame,
His only wish—to serve his country well ?
Of such was Davidson ! The mighty boar
Who dauntless stands amidst the hounds at bay,
His gleaming tusks dimmed with purple gore,
And fiercely fighting gasps his soul away,
Shows not a sterner, more determined, mind
Than Davidson who scorned to turn his back
As all alone within The Crag he stood
And single-handed hurled the foemen back.
And so at last by fearful odds borne down
He fell—and as he fell The Crag was lost.
He clearly gained the brightest of renown ;
Fame is his guerdon—Life the price it cost.

The tall, strong man with the keen, blue eyes standing alone with the weapon in hand to slay as he could each enemy that appeared in the breach caused a second of pause, and they shouted to him to cease fire and he should go unhurt. But the very suggestion was a wound, and he fought until he fell. The enemy was cruel as brave, and had never spared even the bodies of the dead, but they brought in *his* body with all honours.

In letters from the front I was told that when news of the disaster reached camp the sound of Salisbury's voice as he ordered the men to "fall in and follow him" was a thing which no one who had heard it could ever forget. Nor could those who witnessed it forget the glorious charge, straight uphill, that retook the picket. The author continues:

And now we see old Salisbury's "dirty shirts"
Stream up the hill like foxhounds giving tongue
And as the crafty fox astonished hears
Diana's music floating o'er the wind
So the "hurrah" of Bengal Fusiliers
Strikes mortal terror in the Afghan mind;
And so, on this occasion, when they found
Themselves exposed to an alarming fire
With British soldiers swarming up the mound
They thought it was more prudent to retire.

* * *

Far down the hill to bear the battle's brunt
The Sikhs—once Brazier's—show a martial front:
Now Ross commands: the lowest pickets show
Too slight a barrier to the advancing foe:
And the red coats that line that three foot wall
Must e'en retire or only stay and fall.
Some stay. Young Moseley first received a wound
And sank expiring on the crimsoned ground:
The glittering steel waves over Jones' head
And he too now is numbered with the dead.
Chapman has fallen, and beside him lies
Poor Smith, the death film thickening o'er his eyes.
Chapman was much beloved; his men essayed
In vain to save him from the Afghan blade.
He would not move, "Take Smith away," he said,
"For me all chance of life I feel is fled."
"Take Smith away"; and has he spoke he bound
With tender hand his dying comrade's wound.
In Chapman there were happily combined
All the great virtues that adorn the mind—
Noble of Nature, with his patent sealed
By Heaven, and on his handsome face revealed

A trusty friend, a more than generous foe,
And ever mindful of another's woe.
Brave to a fault—and yet how tender when
He saw the sufferings of his fellow men!
What wonder if the angels at his birth
Grudged him a too long residence on earth.

Now Hughes' guns which for awhile were still
Pour forth their volleys from the Standard Hill;
A flanking fire another post supplies
And echoing thunder to the guns replies.
Amidst the sheets of flame and clouds of smoke
Sir Neville called the troops to arms—and spoke:
"Highlanders, follow me, let no man lag,
Honour and glory wait you on that crag."
Forward they press, the general leads the way
To where the haughty Afghans stand at bay.
Sir Neville first is wounded but conceals
Within his iron soul the pain he feels,
Mounts the steep crag—calm is his stern command
Though his pale face betrays his shattered hand.
The picquet taken, he seats him on the ground
And sips his flask while doctors dress the wound:
For seven days more beneath that wound he pines
And then at last—unwillingly—resigns.
Now Garvock takes command, and to his aid
Comes Turner, Commandant of a brigade:
Some reinforcements too had just arrived
And hope once more within the camp revived.

The Village of Laloo.

'Twas now December and the fifteenth sun
Had not as yet his daily course begun
When from our camp five thousand men arise,
Each man provided with three days' supplies—
No tents, no traps, a dire encumbrance prove—
And all is ready for a forward move.
Vaughan with three thousand troops arrangements made
To guard the camp, and there regretful stayed;
Whilst Wilde and Turner their Brigades combine
And forward march in one extended line.
The first ridge gained, the bugles sound the halt
And each man nerves himself for the assault.

Six hundred yards before us, towering, rose
A hill, the main position of our foes.
Sounds the advance—bursts from five thousand throats
A cheer: the echoing rock took up the notes
And hurled them back: the guns their thunder stayed
Pitying the paltry sounds themselves had made.
Our men swarmed up the hill and gained the crest,
Dashed o'er the breastwork—bay'nets did the rest.
Forward they rushed and down to Laloo came,
And mocking wrapped her in a robe of flame.
Lovely she always was—but on that day
She was most lovely as she passed away.
Night, dusky night, who spreads his sombre wings
Calmly regardless of all earthly things
Descend o'er the force: Æolus sent
From his deep cover a blast of air that went
Straight to where Laloo's dying embers lay,
Wafting them far into the night away
Like sparkling fireflies dancing through the groves.
We, in the meantime, gather round the fires
And hope of future fame the heart inspires.
There in the morning, still on mischief bent,
Our troops essay the difficult descent
To where Umbeylah in the valley lay:
Dark tracks of blood the nearest path betray.
De Bude's soul within his bosom burned;
Dangers and obstacles alike he spurned
Despite the steep descent: his Mountain Train
Of guns were soon unlimbered in the plain.
Two Sikh Battalions; Morgan's on the right
And Charley Chamberlain's on the left unite,
These lead the way in line, and sweep the glen,
In all amounting to nine thousand men.
Close by support upon the left appears,
A party of the 7th Fusiliers;
De Bude's guns, and Sappers too combine
With Griffith's battery to support the line.

Umbeylah—be thy evil deeds forgiven,
Thy smoke now rises pleadingly to Heaven.
Three hundred fanatics in anger swore
To see their hearths and home disgraced no more.
As at Thermopylæ three hundred swords

By Spartans wielded dared the Persian hordes,
So here three hundred men anticipate
With rash resolve the slow decrees of Fate.
Straight from the Bonair Pass and sword in hand
They sally forth, a small determined band.
What though the volley which the Muzbees pour
Into their ranks sends to the Stygian shore
Half of their men—the rest undaunted court
The death which they by superstition taught
Believe, will serve as passport to the land
Where dark eyed Houries all expectant stand!
Led by fond hope—they all receive
Such shrift as Muzbee Sikhs are won't to give—
The day was now far spent and Garvock saw
'Twas time the leading Regiments to withdraw
Beyond the Bonair Pass; see! they retire
Covered by Griffiths and De Bude's fire.
That night we wrapped us in our cloaks again
And, weary, stretched our limbs upon the plain.

Farewell! Umbeylah let thy troubles cease.
The Bonair Jirgah comes to sue for peace.
Whilst in prosperity thy very name
Was scarcely known, thy ashes now proclaim
Where gallant hearts are laid.

So ends this unknown memorial. The author does not leave us without a touch of philosophical reflection:

Happy thou who find
Their guerdon in a true and virtuous mind,
And happier still were those whom war's alarms
Left to be clasped in loving woman's arms—
I too was hopeful, but regret to say
I found my lady-love had run away!

Poor Mr. Tucker! But I think his buoyant personality probably was comforted by the heroic sentiment of a far greater warrior:

I'll tear thine image from my breast
And think of thee no more.

I can hardly explain even to myself why I should put in this long interlude about Umbeylah. Though not particularly connected with the chief subject of my memoirs, it is a record of brave deeds such as in his youth he must have been familiar with. Turn from the pages if they bore you. See with your mental vision a narrow, steep, rocky defile, with dark hiding-places on either side, and realize that in that wild, mountainous land this little handful of Englishmen —the embodiment of pluck and daring—went boldly on the path of duty. A brave, but alien and warlike foe was peopling every crevice and cranny of that hidden way. Then remember that *now* the enemies of those times march of their own free will side by side with the men they fought against of old—conquered by the valour, the honest dealing, and the true sportsmanship of our fathers and our sons.

It is a thought worth thinking.

CHAPTER XXI

The Last Chapter

> "The verenation of the past (and to what true heart is the past in that 'Moonlight of Memory' other than sad and holy ?) sorrows not over its departure as one utterly bereaved: the true past departs not."
>
> *Carlyle.*

My record draws to a close.

I spent some brief, happy days at home during 1864-65, but the life was quiet and peaceful leaving little to record.

As before, my Father rode and drove about the country a great deal; it was his chief pleasure. In the evenings we played whist after he came up from his study, where the daily papers had first to be thoroughly digested. Our inconvenient post in those days never arrived until late in the evening. Often guests would be there, but in any case the paper came first! His brother John was still alive and, like my Father, bright and cheery; he liked young company, and enjoyed the best of health, as did we all. We were very fortunate in having no invalids in the family. Indeed, it was so very unusual for anything to go wrong in this way that the slightest deviation was met with a very stubborn, passive resistance to any control, though the doctor was politely greeted, and his points unargued. I remember one very severe bronchial cold when the cough was persistent and proclaimed its need of relief. Though my Father would not go to bed, he consented to remain in his room.

There was a ball somewhere one night, and I took charge and remained at home. My sister never liked to give up her generalship, but she was very young and had been looking forward to this rather rare entertainment—and so she acquiesced. She and Jack went off and left me on guard. My Father's room was large and comfortable and his dinner was served there as usual. When desert-time came he missed the usual ceremonial! He raised his glass and looked at me.

"Sherry," he said (the doctor had particularly mentioned that beverage as a thing to be omitted), so backed by that authority, I said:

"Father, the doctor said it would make your cough worse."

"Sherry," he repeated, "I ask for sherry. Am I master in my own house?"

He never raised his voice but it had a tone which said much! I rang for the wine, poured out a glass, then he tapped the table to indicate that the decanter was to be left. I tremblingly obeyed, but he did not help himself to any more. When the fit of coughing came he said he would go to bed.

Oh! what a night I spent.

He could not lie down, and was very feverish; his cough was distressing, and no remedies seemed to avail. He rambled and talked disconnectedly, but, after a long time and taking my ministrations with patience, he fell asleep just as day was dawning and the revellers returned. He had a fair rest, but nothing would persuade me to relinquish my post. Of course the doctor came, and repeated his injunctions, I said nothing. Dinner-hour came again, and, as I fully expected, we arrived at the same climax:

"Sherry."

I brought the decanter and placed it on the table.

"Pour it out," he said.

I did so, and we looked at each other, I keeping my face as expressionless as I could.

"Take it away," he said in a real commanding officer's voice; but with a twinkle in his eye that was irresistible! I stooped and kissed his forehead. I had learnt that his own good sense was quite enough and that words of remonstrance were provocative.

I think it was on this occasion that the patient was permitted to go down to his study but on no account to venture out of doors. Other members of the family were there then standing in the hall. It was his invariable custom on coming downstairs to walk straight out of the hall-door and have a look round. I do not think he had any idea of being rebellious on this occasion, but unfortunately a masterful hand indicated the door leading to his study, and someone said in playful, insinuating tones: "This way, Father, no going out to-day."

He promptly opened the hall-door and walked out!

No one dared to follow and bring him back. But they cried out to my husband:

"Oh! Jack, do go after him and tell him how wrong it is."

So poor Jack went. He found him walking along quite briskly, and stepped up alongside:

"General, you know the doctor said——"

"Damn the doctor."

Remonstrance ended. He walked all round the lawn, and past the lodge-gate and up the carriage-drive—only his little skull cap on his head.

It did him no harm!

Old age has some drawbacks, and there came a time when he had to consider his diet a little—quite a new line of departure for him, for he was the least greedy man I ever knew. Those about him talked, and talked seriously to him about his duty to himself in supplementing nature by art. It took a long time to make any impression upon him, but ultimately—partly for the sake of a quiet life—he relented. The daughter who had presided over all the preliminaries brought him home with much pride on the day when the seemingly successful achievement was accomplished. She was voluble in her congratulations, no doubt (I was not there at the time), but the principal actor was rather reticent. Next morning at breakfast noticing his reserve she regarded him more in sorrow than in anger.

"Oh! Father," she said, "your teeth?"

It was indeed a parade-voice that replied:

"Look in the coal-scuttle!"

That was the end—except paying the dentist's bill. As I have said, I was not there, but as I visualized the scene I laughed until I cried.

But these three stories are exceptional though characteristic, for his remarks were fuller of mirth than of rebuke. He delighted in the society of his grandchildren and was too ready to condone their faults. Indeed their punishments were kept from his knowledge. It was a matter of great disappointment and annoyance when the extra chair beside him (that was placed as regularly as the dessert was put on the table) was left vacant, and had to be accounted for as a punishment! In those days children came down to dessert, making their ceremonial obeisance at the dining-room door; and he never looked happier than when the house was full of them. Very often they would sing and he would join in, or make them join in his songs, "Drink to me only with thine eyes" and "Believe me of all these endearing young charms." In later years on

Sunday evenings they would sing favourite hymns, and his hand would keep measure with the rhythm.

Some children of that day who are elderly men and women now have still a memory that has come down with the common, old-fashioned, purple, garden pansy with its yellow centre. They remember how he always said in pointing out its resemblance to a face, "Ah! there is my old friend Hagi Khan Kaka." No one seems to have asked who Hagi Khan Kaka was—though we all call the flower by that name still!

When young and active men were round him he became young himself, and shared their joy of life and recalled his own. He seemed able to live again old sporting experiences in the beautiful free, open-air life of his past days, not with sighs and murmurs of regret for past things, but with just a renewal of his old vitality, recalling old names and old friends as if they had never left him.

Before we left Ireland in 1865 we—the family—had removed my Father into a larger house with a fine billiard-table where he could take exercise on those days when his out-door pleasures were impossible. In 1864 Kitty had solemnly made over her charge, according to her husband's instructions, to his sister Anne who, taking Kitty's place, remained with me for 42 years, sometimes in England, but more often with us in India—going backwards and forwards with me four times. As I shall not have occasion to speak of her again I write her memorial here.

She was a handsome woman, and very striking-looking; and in character she was as fine and true and loyal, as she was good to look at. Now, standing on the brink of the eternal river, I love to recall my record of those years when our lives were so intimately linked together, through sunshine and deep, deep, shadow; and I know that, in the beautiful language of the Old Book, she and the other two are of the "*multitude clothed in white, for they were worthy.*"

When leave was up in 1865 two lonely people returned to India. Anne remained with "the baby" whose home was to be with her grandfather and her aunts.

The years immediately following were very clouded, the shadows falling heavily on the dear old home.

In 1866 the Agra bank broke, and everything was altered for the dear Father whom I had left so happily settled. But, thank God, his strength was equal to his day, and except in deep regret for those for whom he had provided so amply it made little change in him outwardly. He had not controlled his financial affairs, leaving them to others who, in doing what they considered the best for him and themselves found to their regret that they had not possessed that business-acumen which is necessary when dealing with banks and investments!

I was far away at the time in Lucknow, but the whole story came out to me and is so illustrative of my Father's character that I record it in full.

One of my married sisters, with her family, was living with him at the time. When the papers announced the disaster and its far-reaching consequences the first thought in all their heads was for Father. How would he bear so great a shock at his advanced age? They did not dare to broach the subject and waited for a sign; none came. Did he know? Or had the notice escaped him? After breakfast the following morning he was preparing to go out for his usual walk in the grounds, and my sister came to help him with his great coat.

"Not that coat, Father," she said. "It wants mending; there's a hole in the pocket."

He changed his coat at her bidding. Then, turning round, said in his serio-comic way:

"What's the good of a pocket when a fellow has nothing to put into it?" And walking out at the door of his fine, big house into the beautiful grounds that surrounded it, he turned round and said quietly: "Look out for a small house at once."

Then they knew that he knew and that these orders must be carried out at once. All his investments had been drawn out and placed in the Agra bank.

But fortunately for him he had the generous pension of the old East India Company to fall back upon. He never complained, or voiced a regret for things he had to do without. The only visible sign of the misfortune was his generous and liberal effort to minimize the trouble for those who had not his resources to fall back upon. In no phase of his long life did self-love dominate or suggest its presence in his actions.

Home was still home to all his children.

After two hot seasons in the plains that had borne their full plentitude of suffering and anxieties a light broke in upon a gloomy day. Jack had been offered a charge at Darjeeling. My anticipations, however, were rather chilled by his decision that his work was too important to leave!

We were then living with my kind brother-in-law, General Beadle, and sharing his house in Lucknow. With his sympathy in all matters he brought pressure to bear on the subject, and all went well!

It ought to have been an interesting journey to Darjeeling, but I remember little or nothing about it until, after a very uncomfortable night-journey in a *dak gharri*, we arrived at a *dak bungalow* (not the *dak bungalow* of my early days !) But the shortcomings of the journey were annihilated when day broke and I saw the snowy range rise, above nearly a third of the horizon ! . . .

All that day I sat with my feet dangling over the steps of the *dak gharri* and sang "Te Deum" with a voice of freedom and a heart overflowing with thankfulness for a renewal of the life that had seemed done for ever. Beautiful Darjeeling ! . . .

The chief incident of my stay there in reference to this Memoir has been recorded in Chapter XII., but I have not yet crowned the glory of those scenes with a word about the monarch of mountains, Kunchinjunga. Our bungalow there stood on a platform facing the snows. This lofty peak is very coy and hidden for months in the year by mists and clouds, but when he does unveil it is with unstinted prodigality. My fortune was very great ; by leaving open a wide door I could see across the valley from my bed. And, in the clear days, at early dawn I could watch the magnificent panorama of sunrise on Kunchinjunga unfolding before my wondering gaze. I have read many descriptions, I have seen many paintings, but nothing I think equals the description of it in these verses by Major F. C. Jonas. He made no claim to be a poet ; he showed me these lines only after many years, when we had been talking over the beautiful things we both remembered ; but no one who has witnessed the pageant would fail to call this not only poetry, but a vivid pen-picture of an unforgettable scene.

SUNRISE ON KUNCHINJUNGA

From Tiger Hill, Darjeeling

By F. C. Jonas.

The night is done; the dawning day glows in the Eastern sky:
The moon must give her Kingdom up and the brightest stars must die,
For the mighty sun with golden shafts cleaves through the darkest cloud
To welcome, with his warning kiss, each peak in its snowy shroud.

Whilst now the topmost mountains stand, their jewelled heads ablaze,
The fleecy clouds take up the light and float in a dazzling haze
Of rainbow hues, so soft, so clear, in colours so divine,
As they slowly drift in the valleys deep and the moss-bound trees entwine.

And now the hidden orb gleams out to hold celestial sway,
And lo! in the vault of Heaven itself, one dazzling golden ray
By Kunchinjunga's loftiest peak is caught in its upward flight,
As in awful grandeur he towers on high, clad in eternal white.

The foot of man shall never tread his trackless, spotless snows;
The eye of men shall never see the sights he only knows;
But solemn and silent, alone, unchanged, from age to age he stands,
His mighty brow in the ether cold o'er-looking the burning sands.

As far-removed from the lower earth as if of another sphere,
From the tainting hand of man he keeps his taintless summit clear;
As a symbol of purity, might, and power, infinite, sublime,
He has stood through countless ages, and shall stand to the end of time.*

* Major Jonas was one of those who joined up when his country called. He was killed in 1917 when leading his men against a treacherous and unworthy foe. I am glad to pay this tribute to his memory. Mrs. Jonas has given me leave to introduce these lines.

The description of the opalescent mist wrapping round the moss-covered trees in the valley and the foreground brings the whole beauty before my backward gaze, as no artist in colour could possibly reproduce it.

My next visit home was to the little house at Ballybrack where my Father's last days were spent. It had a good garden and beautiful views surrounded it. But my husband's relations all lived in England, so that I never settled into this home as I had done before.

About this time my brother Charlie, Captain 50th Queens, after a strenuous time with the Maories in Zululand, came back to Ireland, and decided to take a long tour all over the European countries. It was full of interest and adventure; but nothing could prevail on him to write down his experiences. This was a pity, for he was a clever man and expressed himself in a quaint and original manner. Afterwards, when no longer in the service and a free man, he went further afield and purchased land in Saskatchewan and farmed it. He did a little soldiering too, which was more in his line. He obtained his majority for service in the Riel Rebellion, and was much interested in the early organization of the famous Mounted Police of the North-West Territories.

When Jack returned to India in 1872 all educational arrangements pointed to England, so I settled down there near his relations who became very dear to me and mine and left us happy memories.

In consideration of Jack's services which had been long and valuable—he was now Colonel J. H. Jenkins—he was permitted to remain in the service while holding a lucrative appointment off the line as agent of the Oudh and Rohilkund Railway.

The "baby" had now become entitled to a wider sphere of action, and it was decided that I should take her out to join her Father in the autumn of 1874. Early in that year my sister came over to England for a little change and to help in our shopping preparations; I wanted to pay a long visit home before leaving, and had arranged to get the work of shopping over so that we might return together to Ireland.

But shortly after her arrival we were recalled to Ballybrack.

My Father had unfortunately had a severe fall and fractured one of his thighs.

Of course he could not leave his bed, and must have suffered great agony; but he made no complaint or murmuring. He just lay quite still and spoke very little, but what he did say we have never forgotten. Love and unselfishness, duty to God and man—these had ruled his beautiful life. His example gave weight to his words.

He died on May 24th, 1874, in his 87th year.

Most unfortunately my brother was far away. The light had gone out and our dear home was no more.

But there are lights that can never fail.

It was *his* hand that first drew my childish eyes to the unchanging heaven.

When last I saw his well-loved face
  The Spirit's seal of peace was there
As it left its tent on Earth's camping-ground
  And rose to the courts of the Master's house
With its record, clean and fair.

* * *

Oh! star of the night—thou steadfast star—
With the dear memory of things that were
Blend thoughts of the things THAT ARE.

FINIS